MW00343466

IMAGES
of America

GUARDING DOOR COUNTY
LIGHTHOUSES AND
LIFE-SAVING STATIONS

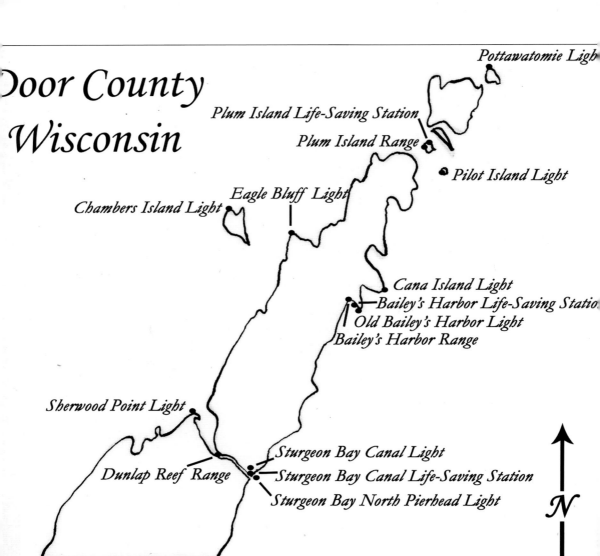

Door County, Wisconsin is the peninsula which juts out of the state into Lake Michigan. The 12 light stations and 3 life-saving stations are shown on this map.

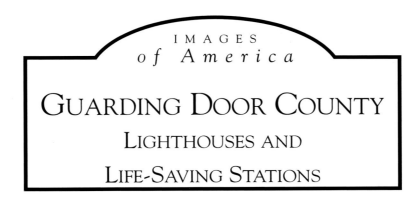

IMAGES
of America

GUARDING DOOR COUNTY
LIGHTHOUSES AND
LIFE-SAVING STATIONS

Stacy and Virginia Thomas

ARCADIA
PUBLISHING

Copyright © 2005 by Stacy and Virginia Thomas
ISBN 978-0-7385-3423-7

Published by Arcadia Publishing
Charleston SC, Chicago IL, Portsmouth NH, San Francisco CA

Printed in the United States of America

Library of Congress Catalog Card Number: 2005923155

For all general information contact Arcadia Publishing at:
Telephone 843-853-2070
Fax 843-853-0044
E-mail sales@arcadiapublishing.com
For customer service and orders:
Toll-Free 1-888-313-2665

Visit us on the Internet at www.arcadiapublishing.com

Dedicated to the men and women of the
United States Coast Guard:
past, present, and future.
Semper Paratus

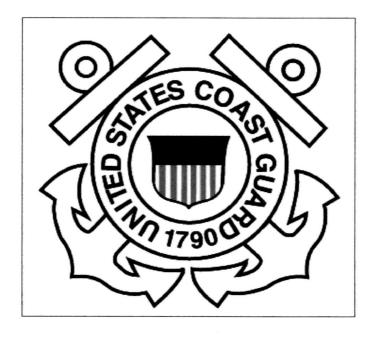

CONTENTS

ACKNOWLEDGMENTS

Research is a unique mix of perseverance, luck, and the kindness of others. Our greatest ally in this endeavor has been the Door County Maritime Museum & Lighthouse Preservation Society in Sturgeon Bay, Wisconsin—specifically June Larson, Doug Henderson, and Brian Kelsey who unselfishly opened their archives and patiently answered our unrelenting questions. Before this project, we had the pleasure of volunteering for their organization on numerous projects and have always thoroughly enjoyed working with them. We also could not have completed this project without the assistance of historians Robert Browning Jr. and Chris Havern of the United States Coast Guard Historian's Office in Washington, D.C. Both were very generous with their time, resources, and expertise. Another great friend to our cause was Tom House who is the Flotilla Commander, Washington Island U.S. Coast Guard Auxiliary, and works at the Jackson Harbor Maritime Museum. Not only did he chauffeur us around Washington Island, but he also dug out the museum from its snow-entombed hiatus so that we could conduct research. We are also extremely grateful for the assistance of the following individuals: Chief Richard Hupf (Sturgeon Bay Canal Station), Tim Sweet (Friends of Rock Island), Nancy Emery and Jeanne Majeski (Door County Library), Karen Newbern (The Ridges Sanctuary), Karen Overbeck & Mary Wendt, Roy Lukes, Kevin Egan (Bailey's Harbor Yacht Club Resort), Kathy Connor (The Eastman House), Joyce Gardner (Pioneer Village), and Sally Treichel (Door County Historical Society). Our gracious editor at Arcadia, Elizabeth Beachy, also deserves accolades for her support, mirth, and expertise. Finally, we would be nowhere without the love and encouragement of our family and friends.

INTRODUCTION

Even though the days of schooners and manned light stations have passed into history, Door County still has an impressive amount of operating lighthouses and maritime traffic. We first became interested in the lights while using them to navigate around the peninsula aboard Coast Guard vessels. Both of us had also been involved in arduous Coast Guard lighthouse painting projects in Manitowoc and Milwaukee. Then came the preoccupation with life-saving stations which grew out of old photographs hanging at the Sturgeon Bay Canal Station where Stacy is stationed. We have thoroughly enjoyed the ensuing adventure of unearthing dormant history and putting it into a format to share with others. We hope you find the stories behind the lighthouses and life-saving stations as enthralling as we have.

Any discussion of lighthouses in Door County inevitably includes a count of lights. By our tally, the county has had 12 light stations. The number could possibly go as high as 16 if ranges were counted as two separate lights, and even up to 18 if one includes Green Island and Peshtigo Reef which fell under Sherwood Point's control in the 1930s. Modern lights, such as the Sturgeon Bay Canal Range, have not been included as they never required a keeper or included a dwelling. We feel, however, that the number of 12 correctly reflects the true amount of historic lights. The chapters are broken up by geographic areas simply because we found that the logical way to work with them.

Range lights, mentioned above, were two lights used in tandem to guide mariners either into a harbor or through a passage. The rear range light would be positioned farther back and higher with a shorter front range light closer to an observer. When the lights were positioned over each other, the sailor knew he was safely in the channel. If the front range (lower) light appeared to either the left or right of the rear range (higher) light, the sailor needed to adjust to get into the channel. Door County had three historic ranges: Dunlap's Reef, Bailey's Harbor, and Plum Island.

Although each lighthouse in Door County is unique, they all followed a general progression. Early lights were lit with sperm oil from whales. When this became scarce, lard oil was adopted. Smoky and easily congealed in cold weather, lard oil was hard to work with. Eventually, kerosene, also called mineral oil, was instituted; it was very flammable, resulting in brick oil houses being built. Then acetylene gas was used at some stations year-round, and in others, just during the winter. Finally, electricity was brought to some lights as they were automated. When the Lighthouse Service was assimilated into the Coast Guard in 1939, some keepers stayed on for a few years, but by 1950, all lights were either unmanned or manned by Coast Guard personnel.

As this tome covers the lights and life-saving stations before and after they became part of the U.S. Coast Guard, some language in the captions may appear confusing. In general, the terms used are time specific so that life-saving stations are called Coast Guard stations after 1915 and their keepers become officers in charge. Most lighthouse keepers had the choice to remain civilian or become boatswain's mates once the Lighthouse Service merged with the Coast Guard in 1939.

To the best of our ability, we have checked various sources to limit any mistakes within this project. We also stress that this is not an all-inclusive history as each light could easily fill its own book. Our goal was to bring to light the overall history of the lights and life-saving stations through the included historical photographs. We are always interested in learning more; please contact us at: stacyrthomas@hotmail.com.

We had the opportunity to gather our resources from many different organizations which are identified in captions by the following:

BHYCR: Bailey's Harbor Yacht Club Resort
DCHSA: Door County Historical Society Archives
DCL: Door County Library
DCMM & LPS: Door County Maritime Museum & Lighthouse Preservation Society
FORI: Friends of Rock Island
JHMM: Jackson Harbor Maritime Museum
LGF: Lumbermill Gallery Framery
LOC: Library of Congress
NARA: U.S. National Archives & Records Administration
NOAA: National Oceanic and Atmospheric Administration
RS: The Ridges Sanctuary
USCG: United States Coast Guard
WIA: Washington Island Archives

One

DOOR COUNTY, WISCONSIN

HISTORY AND INDUSTRY

It is an important public work, involving but a small grant of the public lands to consummate a great public improvement, which, when completed will be hailed with joy and satisfaction, not only by the great lumber interests of Green Bay, but by thousands of shippers, captains, seaman, and shipowners of the Upper Lakes.
— Excerpt from a *c.* 1860s leaflet submitted to Congress in support of the Sturgeon Bay Ship Canal.

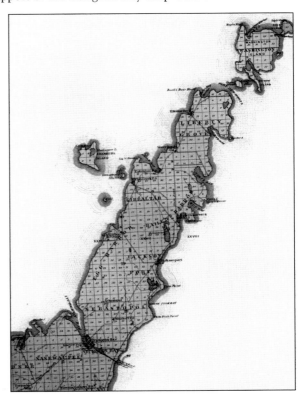

Pictured here is a Door County map from the 1878 *Historical Atlas of Wisconsin*. (Courtesy DCL.)

As a peninsula with many islands, Door County has a strong maritime history by necessity. The lack of roads during its early history meant both people and goods were transported on the water. It wasn't until the early 20th century with the advent of automobiles and quality roads that people began traveling more by land, especially north of Sturgeon Bay.

The first European explorer to venture into this area was Jean Nicolet who made contact with the Potawatomi in 1634. Other indigenous Native American tribes included the Winnebago and Menominee. It is from their traditions that the name Porte Des Morts, Death's Door, became associated with the treacherous passage between the peninsula and Washington Island. According to oral history, around 300 braves trying to cross the passage perished in a sudden squall. The county likewise earned its name from this passage. Fishermen began working the waters around Rock Island in the 1830s, but the first permanent settler was Increase Claflin in Little Sturgeon Bay in 1835. After this, villages began springing up along the peninsula so that by 1860 the region's population was almost 3,000. The growth in population and industry necessitated the establishment of lighthouses and life-saving stations as well as the completion of the Sturgeon Bay Ship Canal.

On October 8, 1871, the great Peshtigo Fire swept across both sides of Green Bay resulting in around 1,500 deaths, although many people claim the total can never been known. The great firestorm is thought to have been fueled by drought, high winds, and smaller fires. The hardest-hit Door County town during this tragedy was Williamsonville, just south of Sturgeon Bay, which was completely destroyed, along with 60 of its inhabitants.

The leading exports during this early period were stone and wood which were transported by ship to various destinations. Shipbuilding also grew rapidly and is still the major employer in Sturgeon Bay. Beginning with Joseph Zettel in the 1860s, many prosperous fruit orchards were planted on the peninsula. The fruit boom occurred in the early 1900s when cherries were the bumper crop; they are still associated with the county today. Farming also took a strong foothold towards the end of the 19th century with peas and potatoes being primary crops. Dairies and cheese production also became more prevalent and profitable and are what most people currently associate with Wisconsin.

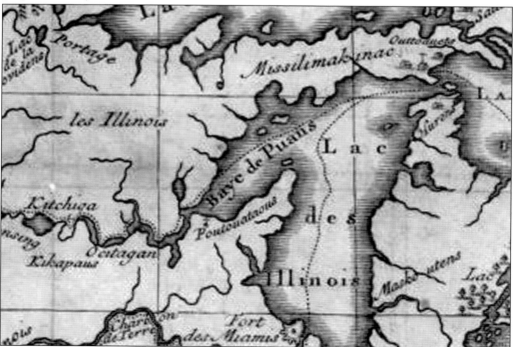

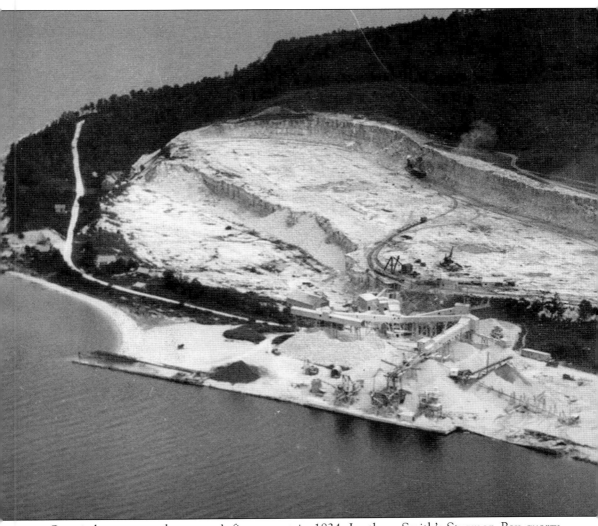

Quarried stone was the county's first export in 1834. Leathem Smith's Sturgeon Bay quarry shown here was founded in 1893 and became Wisconsin's largest crushed stone plant. The quarrying industry petered out during the Depression. (Courtesy DCMM & LPS.)

(*opposite*) The Potawatomi, Winnebago, and Menominee peoples were the indigenous Native Americans of Door County. Jean Nicolet made the first European expedition into Green Bay in 1634. An early rendering of Lake Michigan is shown in this 1737 map of the area by Jean Frederic Bernard. (Courtesy LOC.)

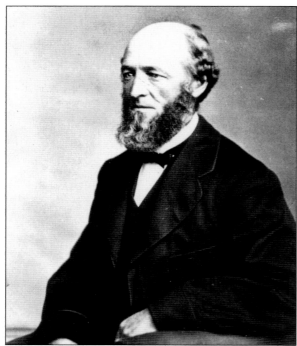

The period between the 1850s and 1870s was the golden age of shipbuilding at Little Sturgeon Bay. Around 1855, Freeland B. Gardner moved to Little Sturgeon Bay and founded a sawmill. His operation grew to include a warehouse, limekilns, shipyard, and docks. His first ship was the *F.B. Gardner*, a brig refitted as a barque in 1866. Other vessels, including the ill fated *Halstead* (see the Plum Island Life-Saving Station section) and the fast schooner *Lake Forest*, were also built here. Financial and fire losses in 1877 led to the end of shipbuilding in Little Sturgeon Bay. (Courtesy Dick Doeren, LGF.)

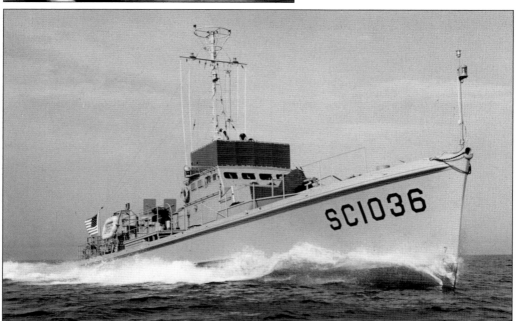

Sturgeon Bay became the center for shipbuilding, especially after the completion of the canal in 1882. Prominent companies include Riebolt & Wolter/Universal, Harris, Leathem Smith, Peterson, Bay Shipbuilding, and Palmer Johnson. Sturgeon Bay played a crucial role in the World War II effort by producing 17 submarine chasers between 1942 and 1944. Built by Peterson Boat Works, the mostly wooden vessels carried a crew of 27 men and were responsible for hunting and destroying enemy submarines. (Photography W.C. Schroeder, courtesy DCMM & LPS.)

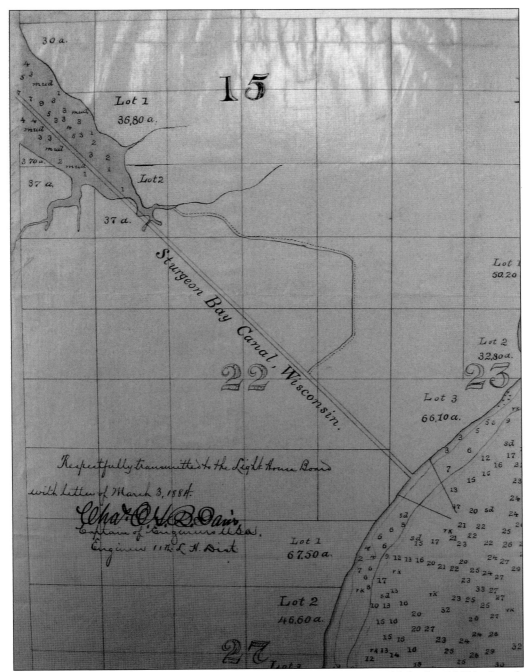

The Sturgeon Bay & Lake Michigan Canal & Harbor Company was established in 1866 by Joseph Harris, Sr., who had established the Door County *Advocate* newspaper in 1862 and had served as state senator 1864–1865. This pre-canal map shows the head of Sturgeon Bay with the canal connecting to Lake Michigan drawn in. The canal was crucial to shipping but also facilitated passenger transport on such vessels as those in the Goodrich Line. (Courtesy NARA.)

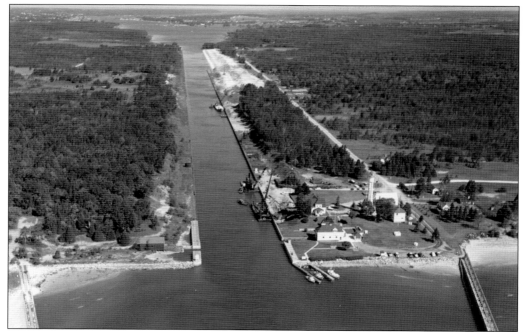

The first shovel of dirt was turned on July 8, 1872. Due to budgetary delays, the canal did not connect the waters of Green Bay and Lake Michigan until June 28, 1878. It was accepted by the U.S. Government in 1881 and opened for full navigation in 1882. (Photography Herb Reynolds, courtesy DCMM & LPS.)

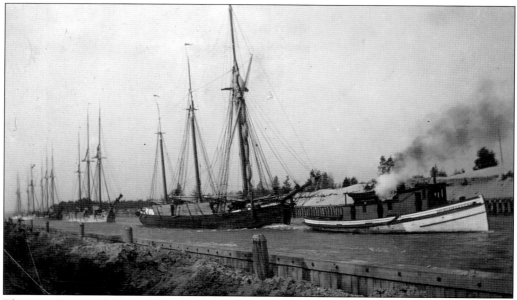

The tug *George Nelson* pulls five wood-laden schooners through the Ship Canal. Lumber exports of maple, beech, hemlock, cedar, pine, and cordwood were a large part of Door County's economy beginning in the mid-1800s. The opening of the canal greatly reduced voyage time and danger by eliminating the need to use Death's Door Passage. (Courtesy DCMM & LPS.)

Two

UNITED STATES
COAST GUARD
OVERVIEW AND UNITS

They will always keep in mind that their countrymen are freemen, and, as such, are impatient of everything that bears the least mark of a domineering spirit. They will, therefore, refrain, with the most guarded circumspection, from whatever has the semblance of haughtiness, rudeness, or insult.
—Alexander Hamilton's Letter of Instructions to the Commanding
Officers of the Revenue Cutters, 1791

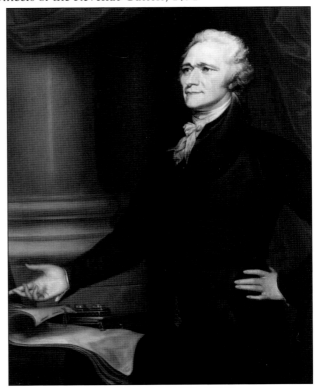

Pictured here is Secretary of the Treasury Alexander Hamilton. (Courtesy USCG.)

It is important to know the basic history of the U.S. Coast Guard to better understand how Door County's lighthouses and life-saving stations now fit within the modern service.

Throughout its circuitous history, the United States Coast Guard has thrived on fulfilling changing and expanding duties while negotiating budget and personnel shortages. Beginning in 1790 with ten boats for tariff enforcement, the service has survived numerous early attempts to become part of the Navy, an assimilation of five separate entities, and the transfer to three different cabinet-level departments. During its evolution, the Coast Guard has faithfully served the American public while performing a variety of missions.

Today's Coast Guard began as five separate federal entities: the Revenue Cutter Service, the Life-Saving Service, the Lighthouse Service, the Steamboat Inspection Service, and the Bureau of Navigation. On August 4, 1790, Alexander Hamilton was authorized by Congress to establish a revenue marine to collect tariffs and enforce customs laws. Called the Revenue Cutter Service or Revenue Marine, it was the only maritime force, as the Navy had been disbanded after the Revolutionary War, and thus holds the proud title as the nation's oldest continuous sea-going service. The Life-Saving Service, founded in 1878, was originally a volunteer organization begun on the New England coast. Sumner Kimball led the reorganization and served as General Superintendent from 1878–1915. Following attempts at assimilation into the Navy, in 1915 the Revenue Cutter Service and Life-Saving Service were merged to form a military service called the Coast Guard. The Lighthouse Service was created very early in our country's history in 1789, clearly showing how navigation and trade were vital to our nation's prosperity. They had purview over lighthouses, lightships, buoys, and minor lights. This service was merged with the Coast Guard in 1939. The last two branches, the Steamboat Inspection Service founded in 1852 and the Bureau of Navigation founded in 1884, merged in 1932 before being folded into the Coast Guard in 1946.

During this varied growth, the organization also moved between three cabinet level departments. From inception until 1967, the service was part of the Department of the Treasury. It became part of the new Department of Transportation from 1967 until 2003. Finally, after the September 11th terrorist attacks, it became part of the new Department of Homeland Security in 2003.

Therefore, lighthouse keepers and life-saving station surfmen who had long helped one another eventually became members of the same organization.

It is also worth noting that the Coast Guard adopted the distinctive 64-degree red, white, and blue stripe in 1967. Furthermore, "working" vessels such as buoy tenders, small icebreakers, and tugs have black hulls, while law enforcement and search-and-rescue vessels have white hulls. Finally, a "cutter" was an English term originally applied to a certain type of small vessel used by the British customs service and adopted by the Revenue Marine. The term is now applied to any Coast Guard vessel greater than 65 feet in length. The following pages highlight Coast Guard personnel and missions.

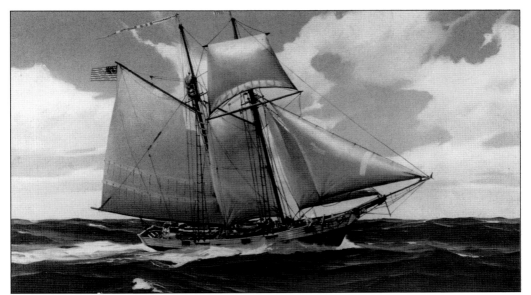

U.S. Revenue Cutter *Massachusetts* was one of the first 10 cutters. The cutter's main duty was boarding all incoming and outgoing vessels to check documentation and ensure the young government was getting paid required duties. Revenue cutters also became responsible for enforcing quarantines, charting coastlines, carrying passengers, and delivering goods to lighthouses. (Courtesy USCG.)

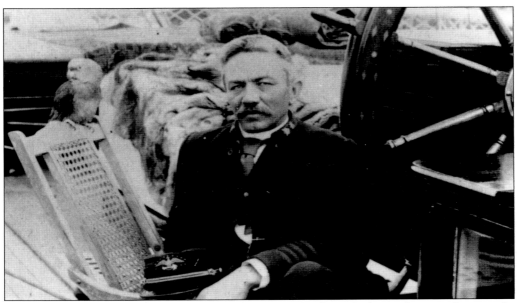

In 1839, Revenue Cutter Captain "Hell Roaring" Michael A. Healy was born as the son of a slave mother in Georgia. His 49-year sea career began at 15 as a cabin boy on a ship bound for Asia. President Abraham Lincoln gave him a commission in 1865, making him the first African-American commissioned officer. He is best known for his command of the Revenue Cutter *Bear* in Alaska, which performed government and humanitarian roles at the end of the 19th century. (Courtesy USCG.)

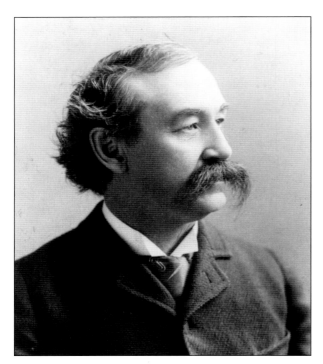

Sumner I. Kimball was the General Superintendent of the U.S. Life-Saving Service from its inception in 1878 to its merger with the Revenue Cutter Service, forming the Coast Guard, in 1915. Due to his shrewd managerial skills, the once run-down volunteer service was transformed into a professional organization of skilled men. (Courtesy USCG.)

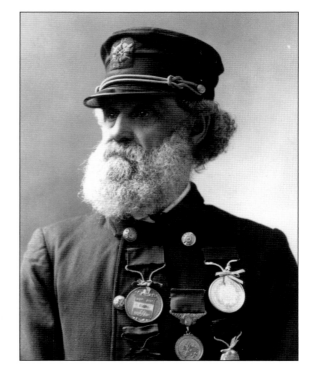

Called "the most celebrated life-saver in the world" by Sumner Kimball, Joshua James was a life-saver for 60 years. During his exalted career, he was credited with saving hundreds of lives off the New England coast. In 1902, after drilling his crew in rough surf, James looked at the sea, said "the tide is ebbing" and fell dead. His coffin was a surfboat. He is pictured here late in life wearing his numerous awards. (Courtesy USCG.)

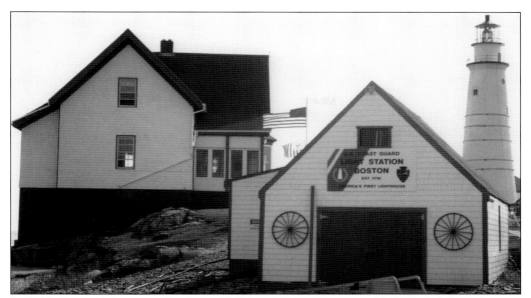

In 1789, the ninth law passed by the newly formed United States established a lighthouse service to erect and repair lights and buoys for navigation. Built in 1716, Boston Light is America's first lighthouse and the only one still manned by the U.S. Coast Guard. The Lighthouse Service became part of the Coast Guard in 1939. (Courtesy USCG.)

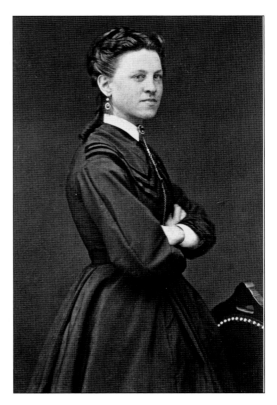

Ida Lewis was an unofficial—and then official—keeper of Lime Rock Light in Rhode Island following the illness and death of her father. Lewis was called the "bravest woman in America" by the Society of the American Cross of Honor for her daring rescues while keeper of Lime Rock Light. Over her 39-year career, she saved 18 lives and was awarded the Gold Life-Saving Medal. In 1996, the U.S. Coast Guard began commissioning 175 foot "Keeper Class" buoy tenders. The first commissioned was the Coast Guard Cutter Ida Lewis stationed in Rhode Island. (Courtesy USCG.)

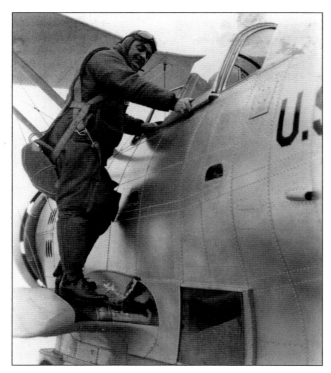

To many, modern Coast Guard aviation may mean the bright orange helicopters seen in rescue missions. However, the first Coast Guard aviator was Elmer Stone who was the pilot and navigator on the first successful trans-Atlantic flight May 8–27, 1919. Stone is pictured later in his career climbing into a Coast Guard Grumman JF-2 V167. (Courtesy USCG.)

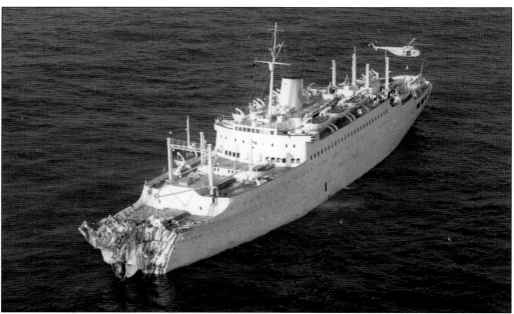

Pictured here is the damaged Swedish vessel, *Stockholm*, on July 26, 1956 after her disastrous collision with the Italian liner, *Andrea Doria*. A Coast Guard helo is at the stern hoisting an injured girl. The collision occurred about 200 miles east of New York and resulted in the sinking of the *Andrea Doria* and the loss of 52 lives. Since the Life-Saving Service began in 1878, the Coast Guard continues to lead in rescue and safety at sea. (Courtesy USCG.)

Icebreaking is an important mission performed normally in the polar regions, Great Lakes, and northeast. Not only is this vital for commerce and navigation, but also for scientists to gather marine science information. The 399-foot Cutter *Polar Sea*, home ported in Seattle, Washington, is pictured here. (Courtesy USCG.)

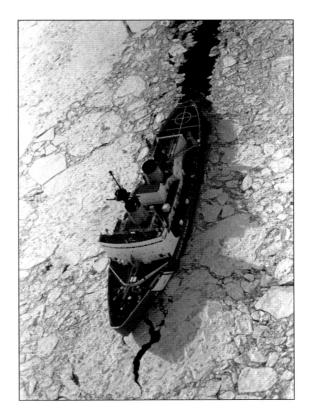

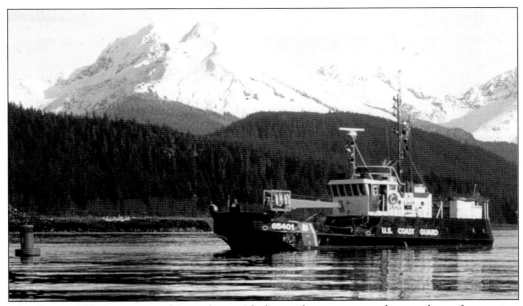

The Cutter *Elderberry*, out of Petersburg, Alaska, makes an approach on a buoy for service. Tending buoys and delivering supplies to lighthouses were duties of lighthouse tenders in the Lighthouse Service until it merged with the Coast Guard in 1939. (Courtesy USCG.)

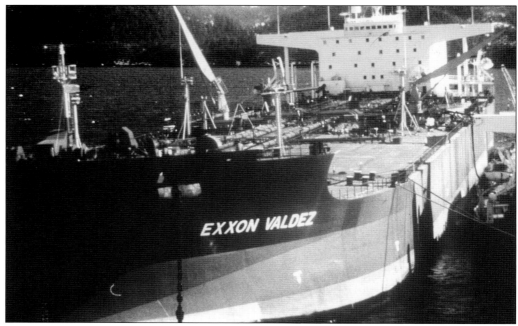

Since 1822, when the Revenue Cutter Service was ordered to prevent the illegal removal of trees set aside for the Navy, the Coast Guard has had an active role in environmental protection. This has included enforcing fishing zones, preventing water pollution, and responding to oil spills. Here is the *Exxon Valdez* aground in Prince William Sound in March 1989, which resulted in a massive oil spill. (Courtesy USCG.)

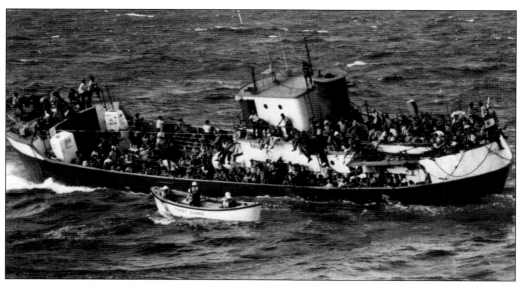

Growing out of its previous Revenue Cutter Service customs responsibilities, the Coast Guard has active programs in migrant and drug interdiction. During the 1980 Mariel Boat Lift, the large exodus of refugees from Cuba to Florida, a launch from the Cutter *Dallas* comes alongside the dangerously overloaded vessel *Red Diamond*. (Courtesy USCG.)

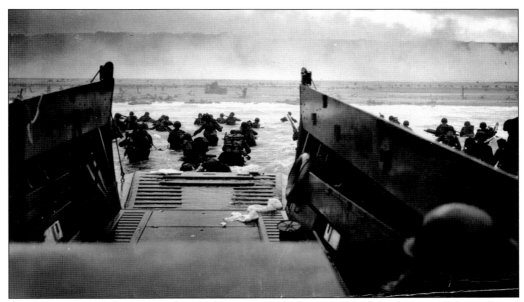

The Coast Guard has been involved in every conflict of the United States. Coast Guard coxswains, small boat operators, were relied upon heavily in World War II for their skill and expertise in surf. This famous photograph was taken on the morning of June 6, 1944 by a Coast Guard coxswain in charge of this landing craft from the *USS Samuel Chase* disembarking troops on Omaha Beach. (Courtesy USCG.)

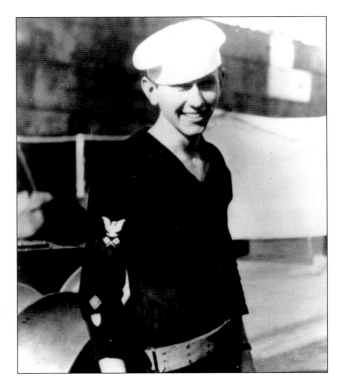

Signalman 1st Class Douglas Munro is the only member of the Coast Guard to receive the Medal of Honor. During the World War II battle at Guadalcanal, Munro was killed in action while attempting to remove withdrawing Marines. He positioned his craft between the enemy fire and the men, all of whom escaped. (Courtesy USCG.)

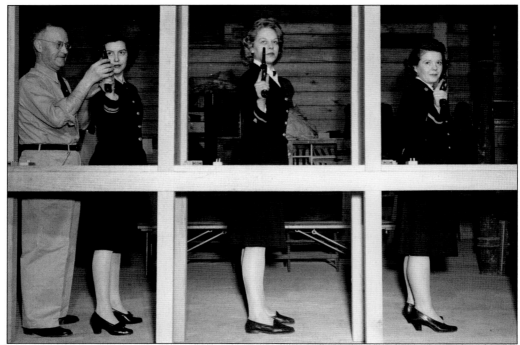

Women first served in the Coast Guard as keepers in the Lighthouse Service in the 19th century. During World War II, the Women's Reserve called the SPARS (Semper Paratus-Always Ready) was organized to fill shore-side positions. Chief Gunner's Mate George Scott gives instruction on the 38-caliber revolver to (from left to right) LTjg Charlotte Wallace, ENS Janet Malloch, and ENS Erna Thompson. SPARs ended after the war, and it wasn't until 1973 that women could serve active duty. (Courtesy USCG.)

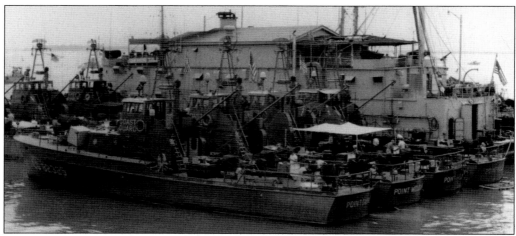

Seventeen shallow-draft 82-foot patrol boats were deployed to Vietnam in 1965 to patrol the coastline and rivers for enemy supplies. On the morning of August 11, 1966, the *Point Welcome* (second vessel in) on patrol was mistakenly attacked by a U.S. Air Force plane, resulting in the death of two crewmembers. The vessel was repaired and continued to serve in Vietnam. (Courtesy USCG.)

After September 11th, the Coast Guard became part of the Department of Homeland Security. New Maritime Safety & Security Teams (MSST) were created to better respond to various threats. MSST 91106 maneuvers their new 25-foot defender class boat in this photograph taken in September 2003. (Courtesy USCG.)

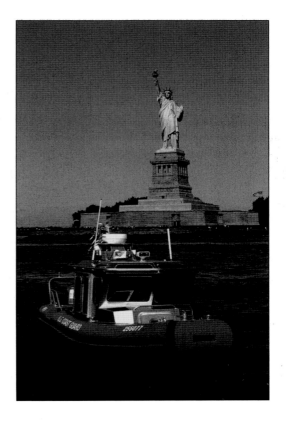

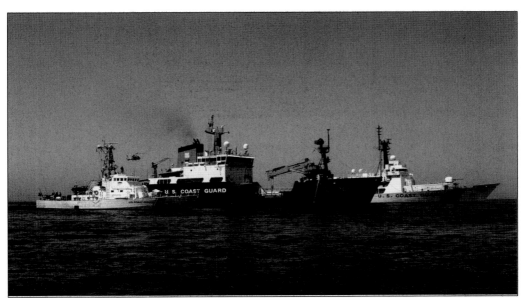

Continuing the tradition of wartime service, Cutters (left to right) *Baranof*, *Walnut*, and *Boutwell* were deployed in support of Operation Iraqi Freedom. (Courtesy USCG.)

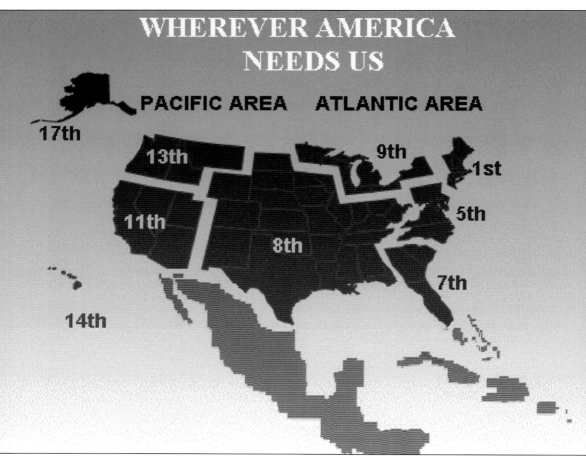

WHEREVER AMERICA NEEDS US

PACIFIC AREA   **ATLANTIC AREA**

17th

13th   9th

1st

11th   5th

8th

14th   7th

This map shows the division of Coast Guard districts across the United States. The entire Great Lakes are part of Coast Guard District Nine based out of Cleveland, Ohio. Within the district are groups which have smaller areas of responsibility. All of Door County is in Group Milwaukee which covers the entire western shore of Lake Michigan. The following units are in Door County and all located in Sturgeon Bay except Station (small) Washington Island which is only operational during the summer: Sturgeon Bay Canal Station, Station (small) Washington Island, Marine Safety Detachment, Electronics Support Detachment Detail, and Cutter *Mobile Bay*. There are also Coast Guard Auxiliary Flotillas in Sturgeon Bay and Washington Island, which are made up of volunteers who support and augment Coast Guard missions. (Courtesy USCG.)

Three

SOUTHERN LIGHTS

DUNLAP REEF RANGE, STURGEON BAY CANAL AND NORTH PIERHEAD, AND SHERWOOD POINT

Lights may be extinguished when navigation is entirely suspended, but must always be shown if it is at all possible for vessels to benefit by them.
—Instructions to Employees of the Lighthouse Service, 1881.

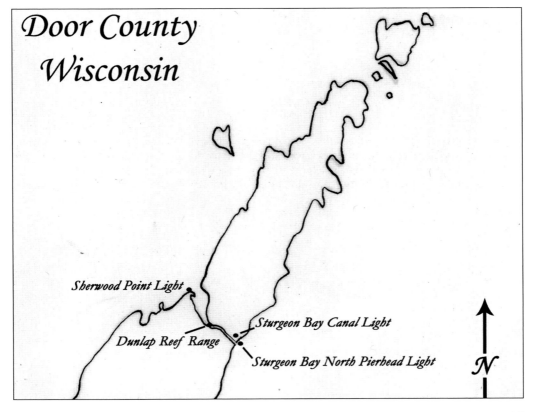

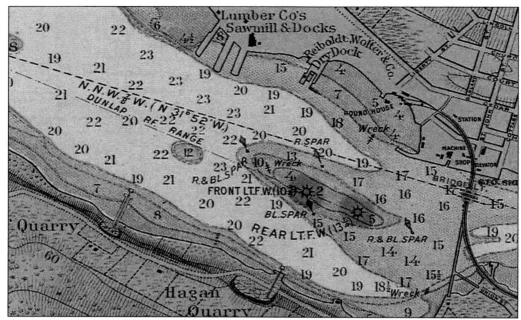

Located just north of the abandoned railroad abutment in Sturgeon Bay, Dunlap Reef, also known as the middle ground, was always a navigational hazard as shown on this 1901 Nautical Chart. (Courtesy NOAA.)

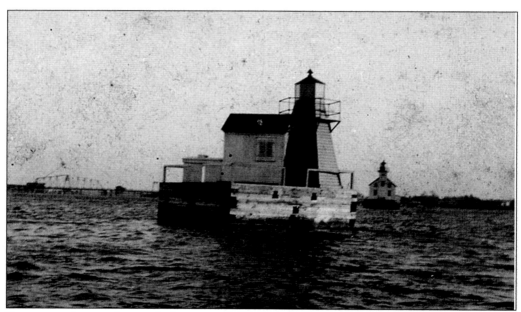

Buoys were first used to mark the area in 1873. In 1880, the Lighthouse Board decided to build a range to guide vessels entering from Green Bay. They were built the summer of 1881 and first lit October 15 of the same year. Here the two structures are shown almost in alignment. The old railroad bridge can be seen in the background on the left. (Courtesy DCMM & LPS.)

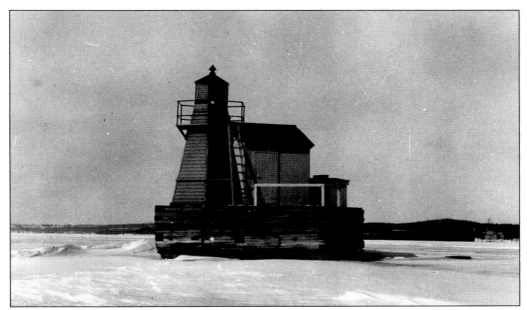

The front range building was four-sided, with a cast iron lantern room on top, and located approximately 700 feet from the rear range. It was white at first, but painted red in 1890. Both lights originally exhibited fixed white lights. In 1907, they were changed to fixed red in order to better distinguish them from the city lights of Sturgeon Bay. (Courtesy DCMM & LPS.)

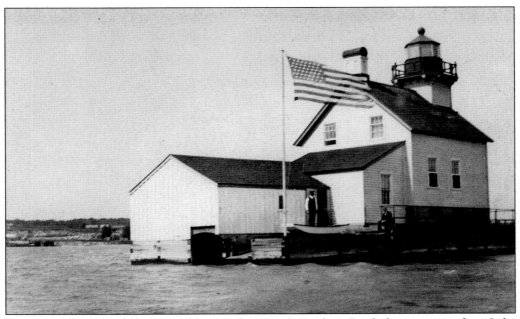

The rear range light was also used by vessels to mark Dunlap's Reef when entering from Lake Michigan. The keeper had to row between the structures at least twice a day to manage the lights. The water level was so low at times (as in recent years) that the keeper could walk between the lights. (Courtesy DCMM & LPS.)

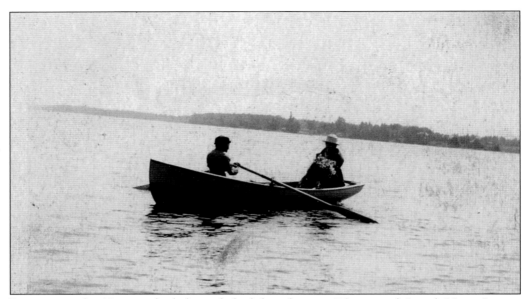

In operation for 43 years, the lights only had three keepers. The second, Joseph Harris Jr., was son of Joseph Harris Sr. who was instrumental in getting government approval for the canal, life-saving stations, and lights. While a keeper at Dunlap's Reef, he began building boats such as this one which gained much fame. The Lighthouse Service even purchased several for other light stations around the country. (Courtesy DCMM & LPS.)

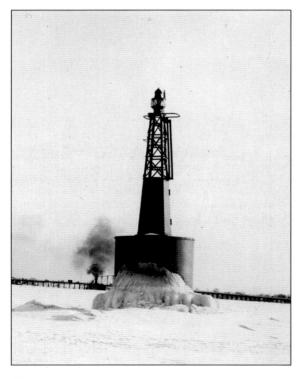

In 1922, the Lighthouse Board recommended the light be discontinued as the wooden support cribs were decaying rapidly and less expensive unmanned lights and buoys could be used. The front range was dismantled while the rear range was moved as a private residence (without tower/lens) to Fourth Avenue, Sturgeon Bay. This acetylene gas light replaced the range lights. It has since been replaced and is currently on the grounds of the Door County Maritime Museum. (Courtesy DCMM & LPS.)

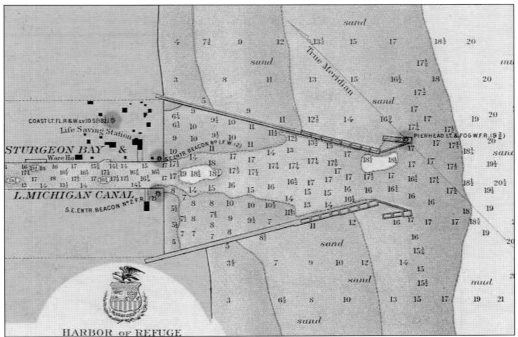

Pictured here are the Sturgeon Bay Canal & North Pierhead Lights as they appeared on a 1901 nautical chart. The breakwaters extend out about 1,000 feet to give protection from both north and south seas. The narrowest entrance between the pierheads is around 300 feet wide. Although the canal was privately built, the U.S. Engineering Department (forerunner of the Army Corps of Engineers) constructed breakwaters. As these lights were not considered separate light stations, they were cared for by the same keepers. (Courtesy NOAA.)

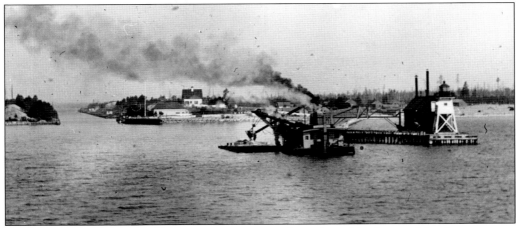

The original north pierhead structure was an exposed wooden white frame with a lantern room atop completed in 1882 by Charles Dobson. The 6th order Fresnel lens first displayed a fixed red light May 15, 1882. The first keeper, Rufus M. Wright, lived on a Canal Company dredge while his family remained in Fish Creek. He was removed before the Canal Light and keeper's dwelling were built. This c. 1890 photograph shows the original tower with a fog signal building added in 1884. A 5th order lens was installed in 1900. (Courtesy DCMM & LPS.)

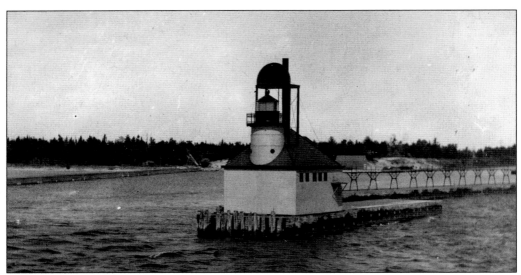

Due to rapid deterioration of the wooden frame and fog signal machinery, the entire structure was rebuilt in 1903. The new white building, pictured here in July 1913, housed both the light and the steam powered fog whistles. (Courtesy USCG.)

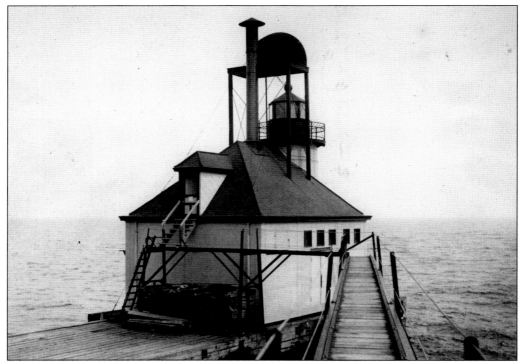

The labor-intensive care required by the steam-powered fog whistle included maintaining complicated machinery, keeping wood ready for burning, and operating the signal day or night whenever fog was present. To help with these extra responsibilities, the Lighthouse Board added an assistant keeper when the first fog signal was built in 1884. This picture was taken in 1914. (Courtesy USCG.)

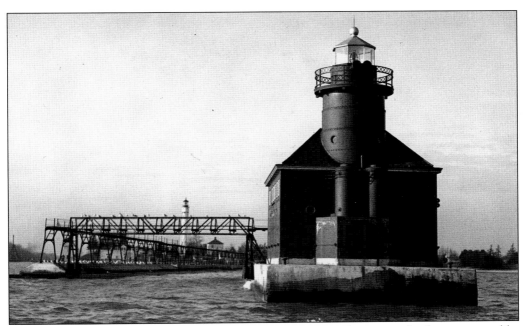

In the late 1920s, the steam-powered fog whistle was converted to an air diaphone powered by air compressors and engines. These were easier to operate and maintain. With this change, the obsolete directional hood previously mounted above the light was removed. The structure was repainted red sometime between 1925 and 1940. (Courtesy USCG.)

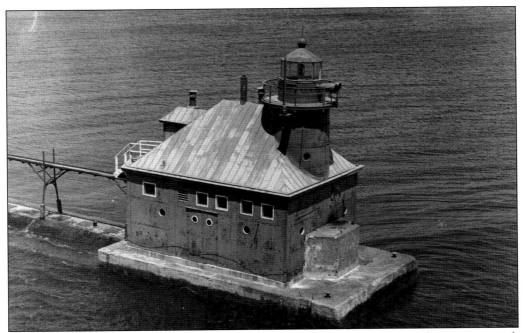

Eventually, electricity was used to power the fog signal, and the exterior air tanks were removed. This 1940 picture shows the light much as it appears today. (Courtesy USCG.)

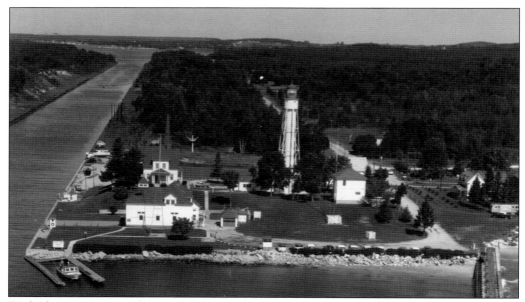

With the growing popularity of the canal came the demand for a stronger light at the Lake Michigan entrance. The Sturgeon Bay Canal Light was built in 1898, housing a 3rd order rotating Fresnel lens which displayed an alternating red and white flash pattern with a range of 18 miles. (Courtesy USCG.)

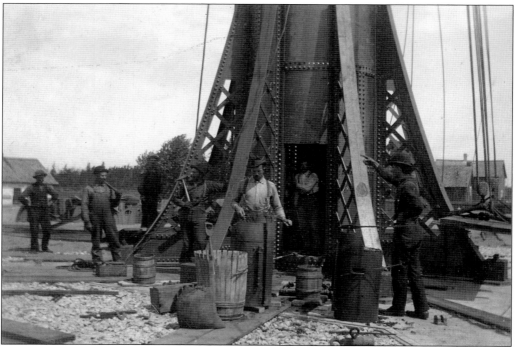

The tower was originally painted brown while the lantern was black. There were eight buttresses which extended sixteen feet up the tower and six feet out from the base. Unfortunately, this would not be stable enough to prevent vibrations. (Courtesy DCMM & LPS.)

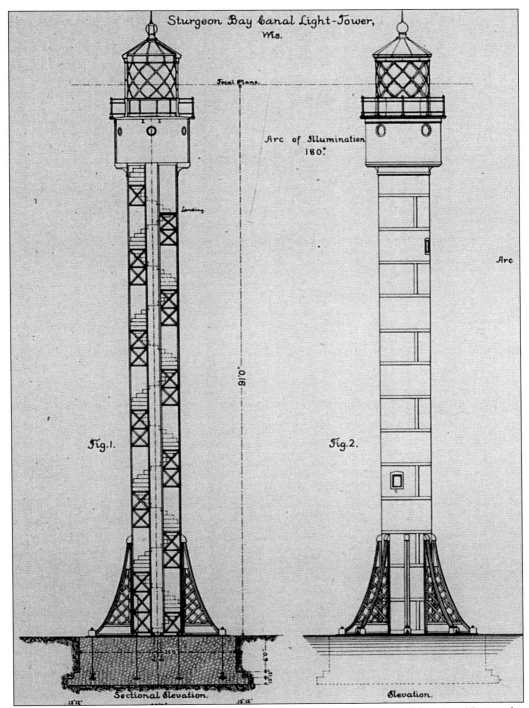

Sturgeon Bay Canal Light-Tower, Wis.

Focal Plane.

Arc of Illumination 180°.

Landing

Arc

91'0"

Fig.1.

Fig.2.

Sectional Elevation.

Elevation.

Pictured above is an original 1898 architectural drawing, sans the external framing. Notice the diamond-shaped panes in the lantern room which were curved glass to help reduce reflections. (Courtesy NARA.)

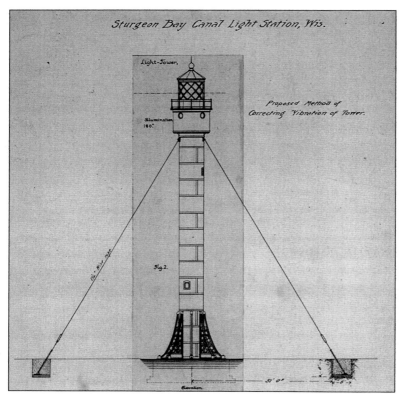

Almost immediately, it became obvious the tower was not built to withstand local winds. The vibrations did not allow the clockwork mechanism that rotated the lens to operate correctly. The first solution was the use of guy wires as illustrated in this 1899 proposal. (Courtesy NARA.)

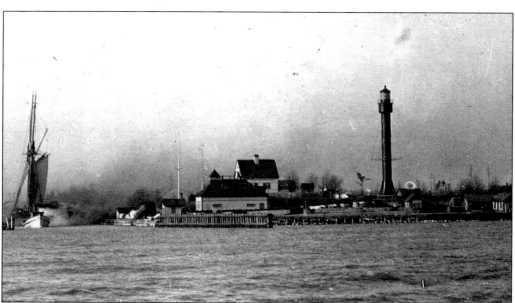

A solution was executed in December 1898, a few short months after the completion of the light. Even with guy wires installed, the light continued to vibrate in the wind. The wires also expanded and contracted due to the amount of heat on either side of the tower, which would cause the tower to list. (Courtesy DCMM & LPS.)

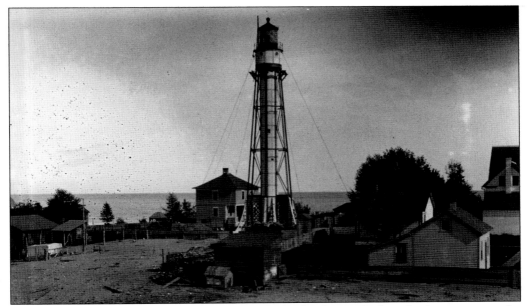

Due to complaints of mariners who said they had a hard time finding the brown tower, the tower was repainted white in 1900. In 1903, the Lighthouse Board constructed a steel skeletal frame around the tower. This finally corrected the vibrations and allowed the clockwork mechanism to function properly. (Courtesy USCG.)

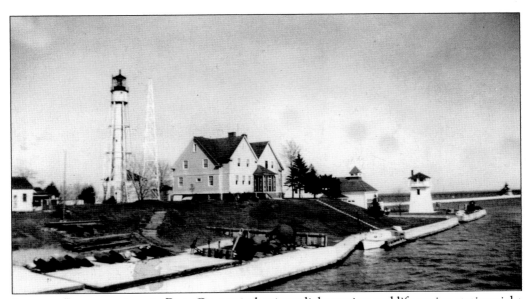

Sturgeon Bay was unique in Door County in having a light station and life-saving station right next to each other. The keeper's dwelling in the center sometimes housed personnel from both stations. Also visible is the keeper's boat slip and launch. (Courtesy DCMM & LPS.)

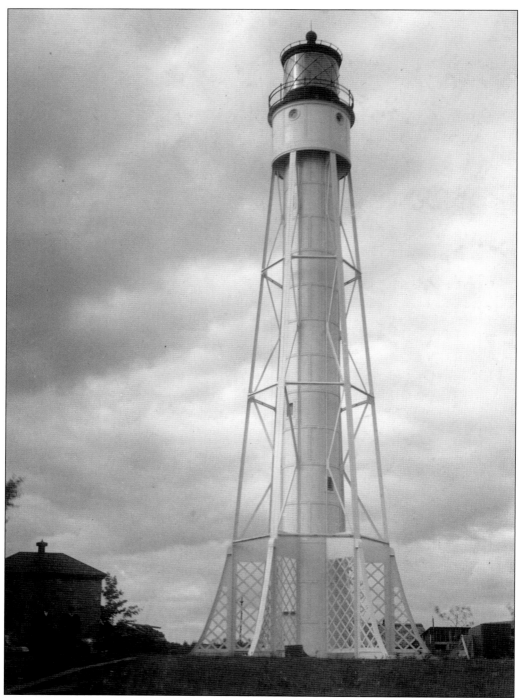

This 1903 picture shows the tower once the support bracing was completed. The two unidentified gentlemen at the lower left may be Keeper Charles Chapman and First Assistant Charles Bavry. (Courtesy USCG.)

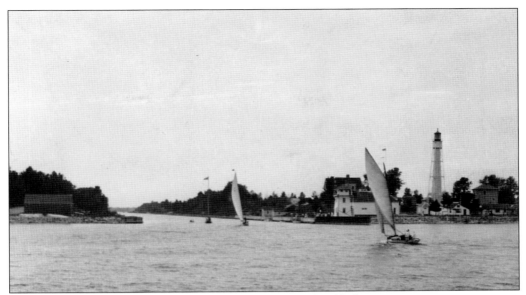

With a focal plane of 107 feet, the alternating white and red light was a prominent navigation aid and used by many boaters. This characteristic was changed to a 10-second red flash sometime between 1957 and 1975. (Courtesy DCMM & LPS.)

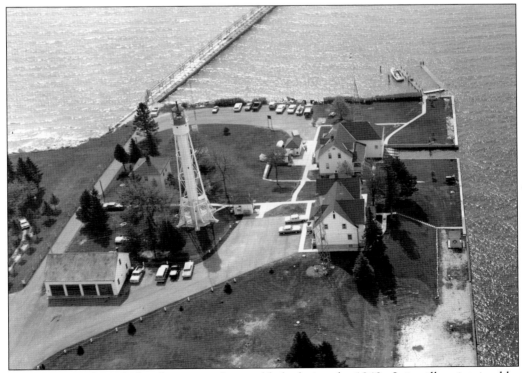

The light was electrified and automated, most likely during the 1940s. It is still maintained by Coast Guard personnel as an important aid to navigation. (Courtesy USCG.)

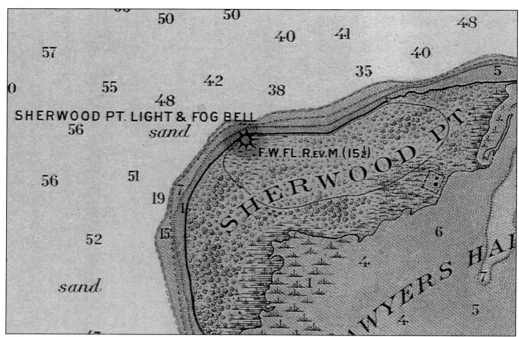

Sherwood Point Lighthouse is shown here on a 1901 nautical chart. The point was named for an early settler, Peter Sherwood. (Courtesy NOAA.)

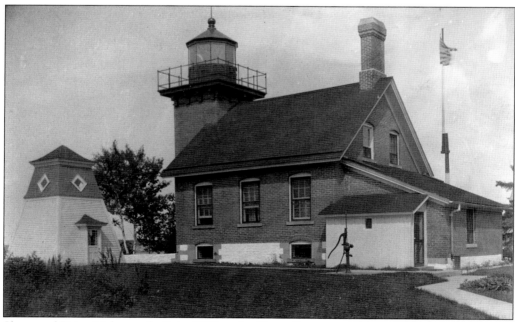

Sherwood Point Light was built in 1883 at the Green Bay entrance into Sturgeon Bay. It is the only Door County lighthouse constructed of red brick obtained from the lighthouse depot in Detroit instead of Milwaukee. The one-and-a-half story structure, square tower, and kitchen attached on the right are shown here as they appeared in July 1913. (Courtesy USCG.)

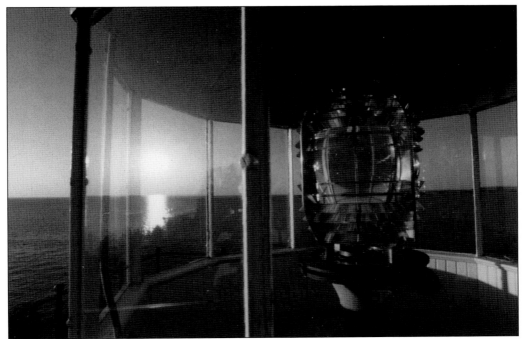

The original 4th order lens was replaced in 1898 with this 1880 4th order lens previously used in Passage Island Light, Lake Superior. Henry Stanley, the first keeper, had a frustrating time maintaining the intricate clockworks which produced a fixed white light with a red flash every minute. This lens was replaced in 2002 with a 300-millimeter lantern and is on display at the Door County Maritime Museum. (Courtesy DCMM & LPS.)

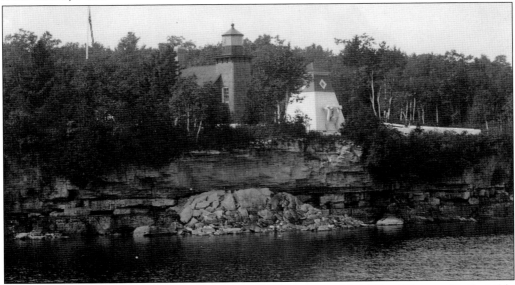

In the summer of 1892, the pyramidal fog signal building was added. The 600-pound bell visible in this August 1914 photograph was automated to sound once every twelve seconds—however, the clockworks mechanism had to be wound every four hours while in use. (Courtesy DCMM & LPS.)

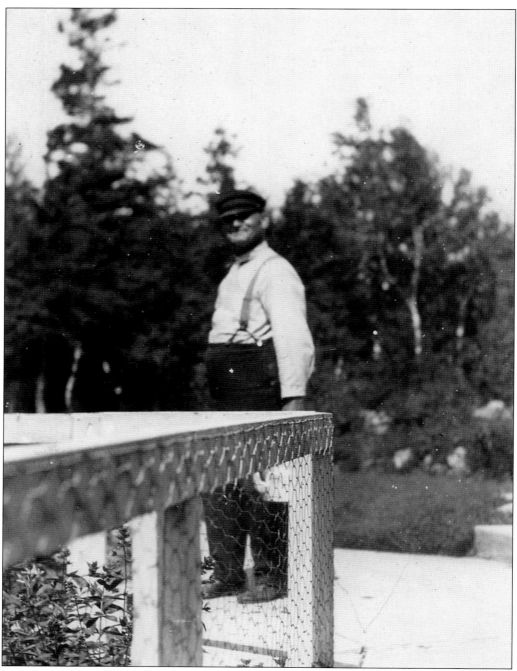

In 1889, William Cochems married Minnie Hesh, niece of Keeper Henry Stanley. Cochems became assistant keeper in 1895, and keeper upon Stanley's death five months later. The second of the only three civilian Sherwood Point Light keepers, Cochems served almost 39 years, accomplishing the longest service of any Door County keeper at a single light. Great-great grandson, LCDR Tim Wendt, continues a family tradition of Coast Guard service as commanding officer of the Cutter *Oak* in Charleston, South Carolina. (Courtesy Mary Wendt.)

Although she had already performed keeper duties for years, Minnie officially became an assistant keeper in 1898. She died suddenly of an apparent heart attack at the light in 1928. Many visitors claim to have experienced visits from her benevolent spirit. (Courtesy Mary Wendt, great granddaughter.)

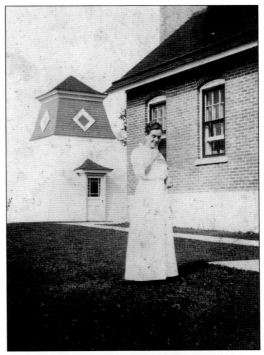

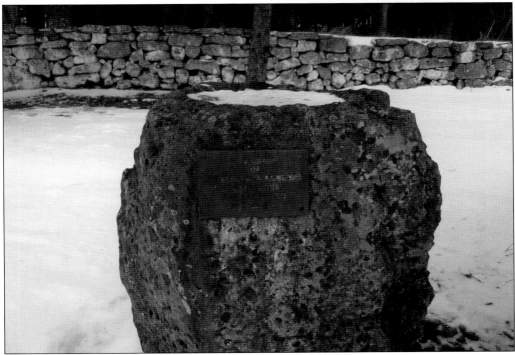

William Cochems erected this stone birdbath and a plaque still present at the lighthouse which reads: "In memory of Minnie Hesh Cochems / Assistant Light-Keeper 1898–1928." (Authors' Collection.)

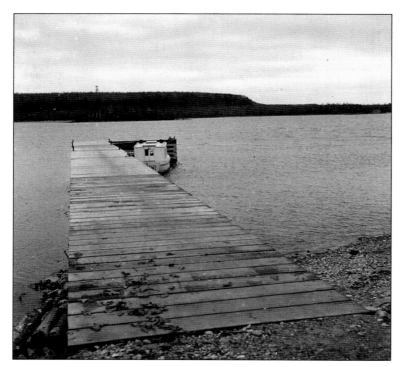

The keeper's boat dock was built in 1885 and located in protected Sawyer Harbor on the opposite side of Sherwood Point. The keepers used this dock to get to and from the city, check on Peshtigo and Green Island lights, and sometimes land supplies for the Sherwood Point Light. The Potawatomi State Park lookout tower can be seen rising above the tree line in the distance. (Courtesy USCG.)

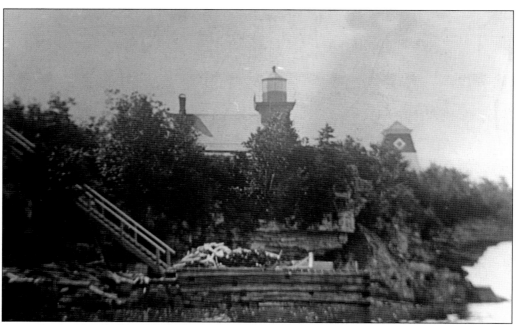

A new landing was built in 1891 with steps which led up the bluff. This allowed lighthouse tenders to directly unload supplies without first having to transfer them to shallow-draft vessels. Exposed to the elements, this new landing wasn't conducive for storing the keeper's launch. On the far right is the outcropping called "lover's leap," which collapsed in 1912. (Courtesy DCMM & LPS.)

Anton Jessen Jr. is show here during his tenure with the Lighthouse Service which he joined in 1930. He served at Chicago, Wind Point, Racine, Sherwood Point, and Sturgeon Bay Canal lights. He was keeper at Minneapolis Shoal for ten years and Manistique for two years. His father, Anton Jessen Sr, joined the Life-Saving Service in 1898, served at Plum Island, and was eventually Officer in Charge of Station Kewaunee. (Courtesy DCMM & LPS.)

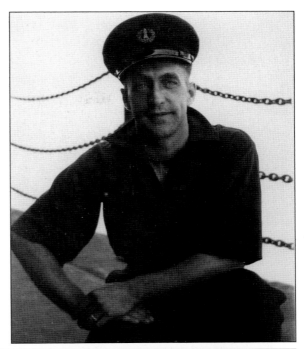

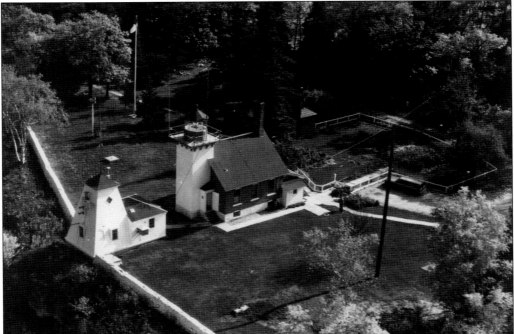

Many changes occurred during the 1930s. Electricity was installed to power the light, a fog horn (the bell was removed), and a radio. A radio room, shown here on the back of the fog signal building in 1966, was added; the keeper used it to transmit weather and contact other units. Sherwood Point was the last manned light on the Great Lakes when it was finally automated in 1983. (Courtesy USCG.)

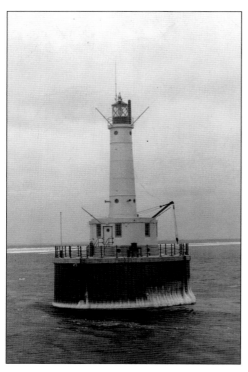

Located eight-and-a-half miles to the northwest, Peshtigo Reef Light marks a dangerous shoal which juts out from the land. First marked by a light ship, the light station pictured here was built in 1935. The light was automated, but the Sherwood Point Keeper had to activate the fog signal by radio control and service the station. Eventually the fog signal was also automated and a red horizontal stripe was painted around the tower. (Courtesy DCMM & LPS.)

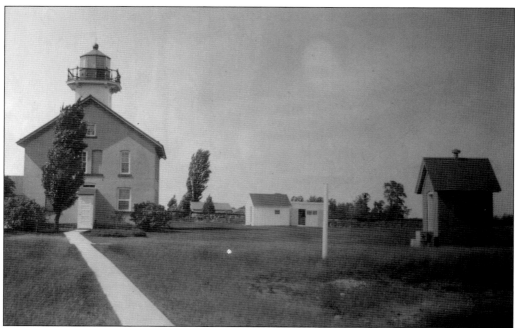

Green Island Light, located 12 miles north northwest, was likewise automated around 1935 and put under the care of the Sherwood Point Keeper. A steel tower with a beacon was built in the 1950s and the main building has since been reduced to ruins. The light is shown here in 1883. (Courtesy NARA.)

Four

Northern Lights

Old Bailey's Harbor, Bailey's Harbor Range, Cana Island and Eagle Bluff

Wind northeast, most terrific gale for years. The grounds and house flooded with water. The sea breaking over the bank and all around the dwelling. The bank on the NE side torn away by the force of the sea.
  —Keeper William Sanderson, Cana Island Log, November 17, 1885

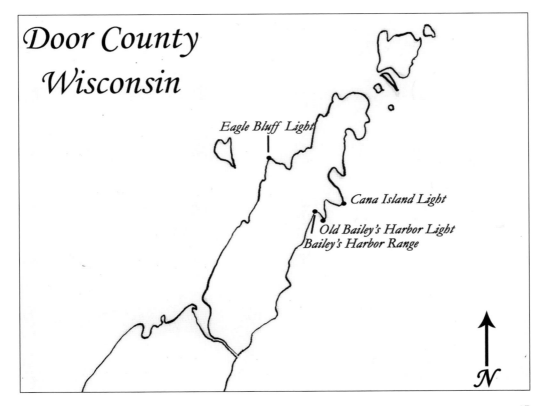

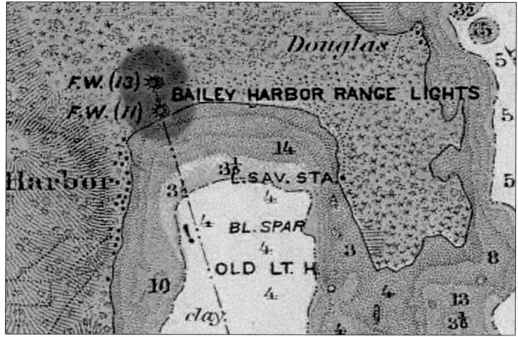

This 1910 nautical chart shows the Bailey Harbor Range Lights as well as its abandoned forerunner. (Courtesy NOAA.)

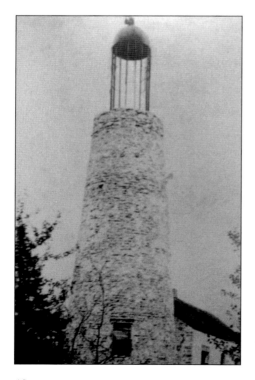

Bailey's Harbor is named for Captain Justice Bailey who sought shelter in the port in 1848. Informed of the area's resources, his employer, Alanson Sweet, quickly set up a sawmill and a stone quarry and petitioned Congress for a lighthouse. Old Bailey's Harbor Light is known affectionately as the "birdcage" due to its distinctive and rare lantern room. Built in 1852 with local limestone, the light was not placed in the best location to guide mariners into the harbor. It was discontinued in December 1869, but is still standing. (Courtesy Roy Lukes.)

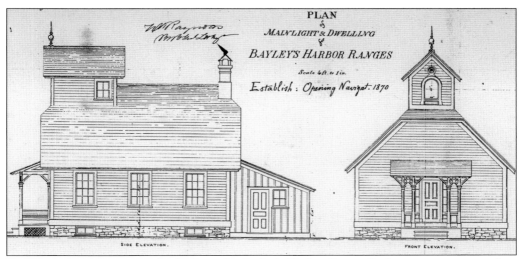

PLAN
of
MAIN LIGHT & DWELLING
of
BAYLEY'S HARBOR RANGES
Scale 4ft. to 1 in.
Establish: Opening Navigat. 1870

SIDE ELEVATION.

FRONT ELEVATION.

To better guide ships into the harbor, the Bailey's Harbor Range Lights were constructed in 1869. Located at the head of the bay, the lights were much better positioned to help the mariners avoid the numerous shoals and rocks in the area. The rear range was a one-and-a-half story white-clapboard structure with the lens located in the cupola on top. (Courtesy RS.)

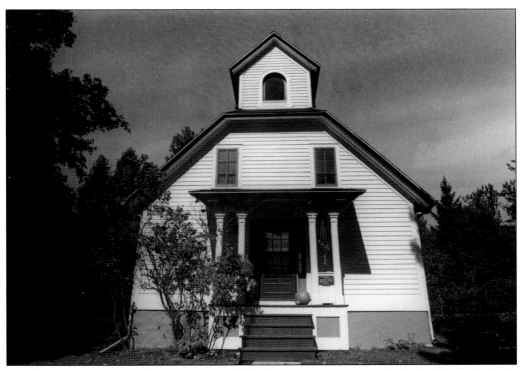

First lit at the opening of navigation in 1870, the range was originally fueled by lard oil. In 1880, the use of the more manageable kerosene was instituted. Eventually this was replaced by acetylene gas and then finally electricity. The rear range housed a 5th order Fresnel lens. (Courtesy DCMM & LPS.)

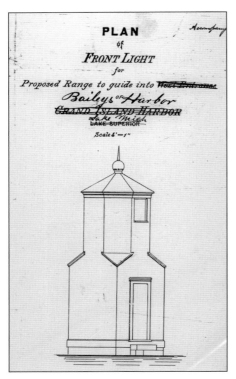

PLAN
of
FRONT LIGHT
for
Proposed Range to guide into ~~West Entrance~~
Baileys or Harbor
~~GRAND ISLAND HARBOR~~
Lake Mich.
LAKE SUPERIOR
Scale 4'—1"

The front range was located approximately 950 feet south of the rear range. The 21-foot high white wooden structure was square at the base, and then octagonal around the lens. This architectural drawing was originally for Grand Island Range in Michigan, whose original wooden structures have since been replaced by metal towers. (Courtesy RS.)

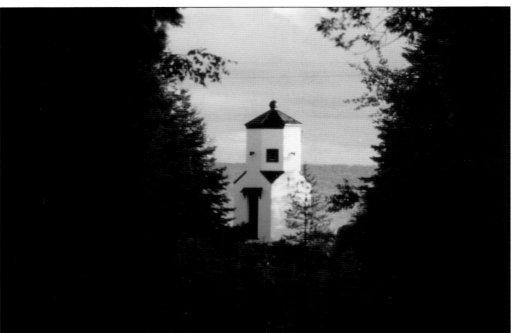

Pictured here is a view of the front range, looking toward the harbor. The small window in the back of the structure allowed the keeper to ensure the light was burning without having to go physically check it himself. (Courtesy DCMM & LPS.)

Keeper Henry Gattie stands on the right, in his keeper's uniform, beside an unidentified gentleman. Gattie was keeper from 1896 until the light was put under the care of the Cana Island Keeper in 1923. He later served at Two Rivers Light and eventually retired after 45 years of service. (Courtesy RS.)

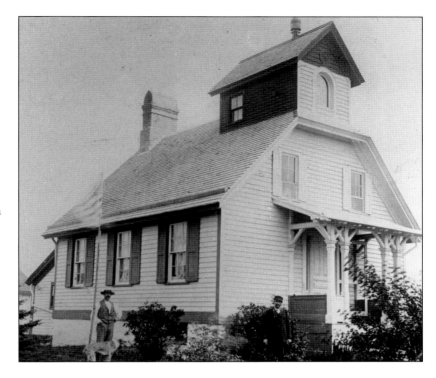

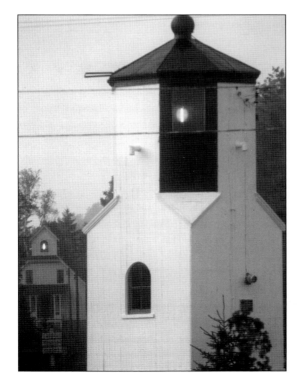

Due to the Sturgeon Bay Ship Canal and improving roads, Bailey's Harbor saw less and less commercial traffic. In 1923, the lights were converted to acetylene gas lamps with an automatic device which eliminated the need for an onsite keeper. The Cana Island Keeper was then made responsible for monthly maintenance and any emergency care. The lights were electrified in 1930 and were replaced by a single leading light on a steel tower around 1970. The wooden structures remain and are now part of The Ridges Sanctuary. (Courtesy DCMM & LPS.)

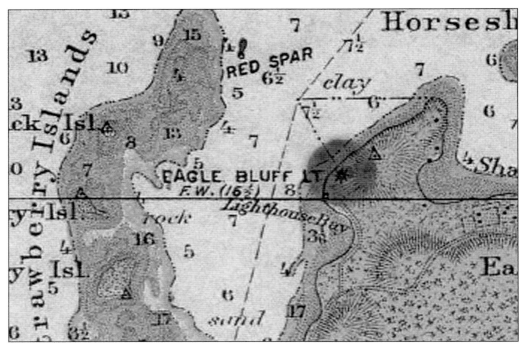

Eagle Bluff Light, as shown on this 1910 nautical chart, sits on the edge of a steep bluff. Supplies were offloaded just south at the protected Lighthouse Bay which had a lower elevation. (Courtesy NOAA.)

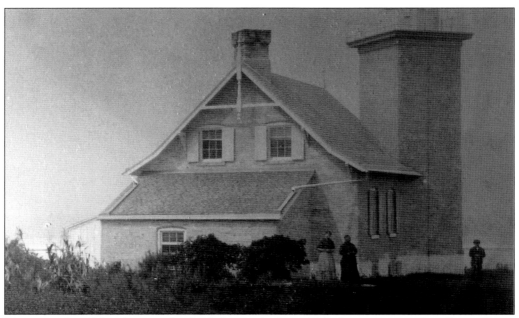

Shown in this 1883 photograph, the light was built in 1868 due to increased traffic in Green Bay. It was situated to help vessels using the passage between Door County and Chambers Island. It was built of the famous Milwaukee cream-colored brick. (Courtesy NARA.)

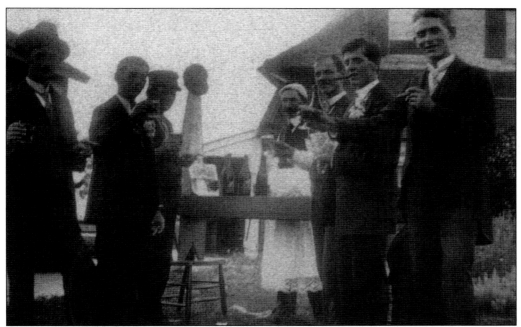

William Duclon served 35 years as keeper of the light, from 1883–1918. His boisterous family of seven boys were helpful with upkeep of the grounds and were renown fishermen as well as musicians. The eldest, Ambrose, was even a member of the Sturgeon Bay Life-Saving Station in the 1890s. The Duclon family is pictured here during the wedding of Charles Duclon to Edith Ehrke at the light on September 8, 1900. (Courtesy DCHSA.)

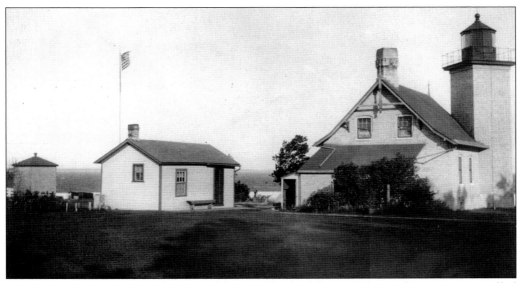

The light housed a 3 1/2 order Fresnel lens and lard oil lamp. Kerosene lamps were installed in March 1881, yet the brick oil house located on the far left was not built until 1900. The building between the dwelling and oil house is a summer kitchen added in 1898. In this c. 1914 image, notice how the chimney is positioned to mimic the tower which was constructed diagonally to the main structure. (Courtesy USCG.)

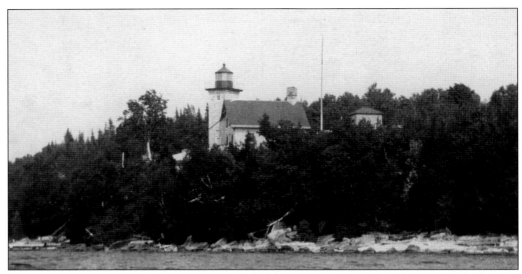

This 1919 photograph clearly shows the high bluff on which the lighthouse was built. The focal plane of the light was 76 feet above the lake level. In 1917, a brighter incandescent oil vapor lamp was installed. The stronger light warranted a weaker lens, and a 5th order lens was installed the following year. (Courtesy DCMM & LPS.)

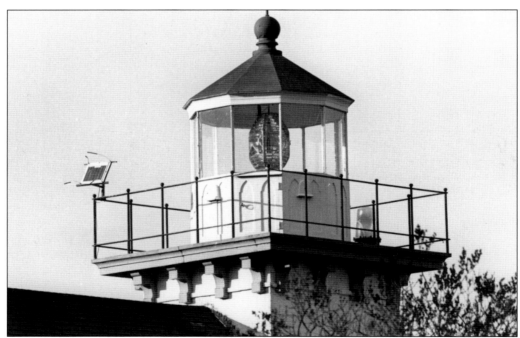

Like Bailey's Harbor Range three years prior, this light was converted to an unmanned acetylene gas light under the supervision of the Cana Island crew in 1926. It was eventually electrified and the lens, although present, is no longer lit. Instead, the Coast Guard maintains the 300-millimeter lantern located on the right of the lantern room in this picture as an active aid to navigation. (Courtesy DCMM & LPS.)

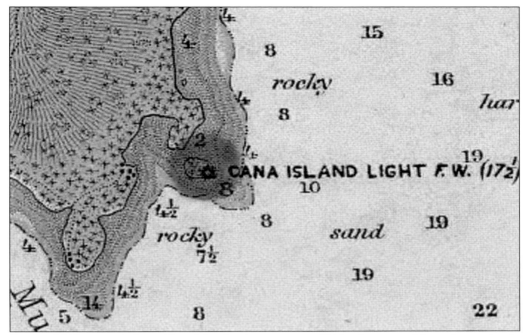

On this 1910 nautical chart, Cana Island is shown as a small island separated from the peninsula by about 300 feet of very shallow water. (Courtesy NOAA.)

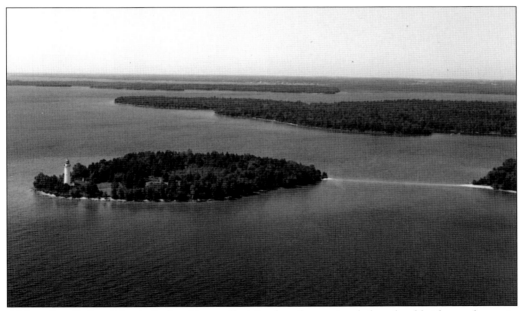

Although called an island, the land is usually joined to the peninsula by a land bridge as shown in this aerial photograph. At times the bridge would be covered by water; other times it would be dry and vehicles could drive across it. In 2004 it was the latter, and we drove our own truck across it to the light to conduct preservation projects with the DCMM & LPS. (Courtesy DCMM & LPS.)

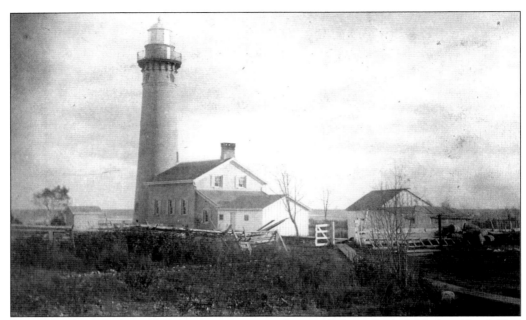

Cana Island was built in 1869 to act as an approach coast light to Bailey's Harbor, North Bay, and Moonlight Bay (also called Mud Bay). The tower and dwelling were constructed with Milwaukee cream brick on the east end of the almost nine-acre tract. A 3rd order Fresnel lens illuminated a fixed white light for the first time in January 1870. This *c.* 1890s picture shows the original brick tower. (Courtesy DCMM & LPS.)

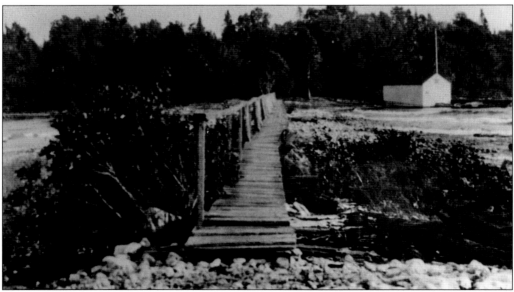

This wood footbridge, first built in 1890 while William Sanderson was keeper, gave a little easier access to the mainland, especially whenever the water level rose. Over the years, the original bridge was damaged by storms but regularly repaired until 1925 when it was dismantled. Keepers and their family members often walked to nearby Bailey's Harbor (four miles) for business and recreation. (Courtesy DCMM & LPS.)

Due to heavy weather, the brick on the tower was rapidly deteriorating. In 1902, steel plates were riveted around the brick tower and cement was poured in the space between. The new exterior was given the gleaming white appearance for which it is well known today. Here, a crew paints the exterior in an image taken in 1902 when the new exterior was installed or possibly during regular maintenance at a later time. (Courtesy DCMM & LPS.)

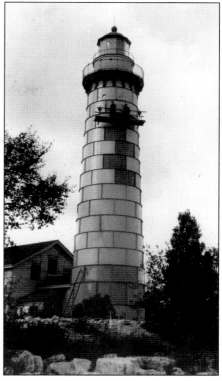

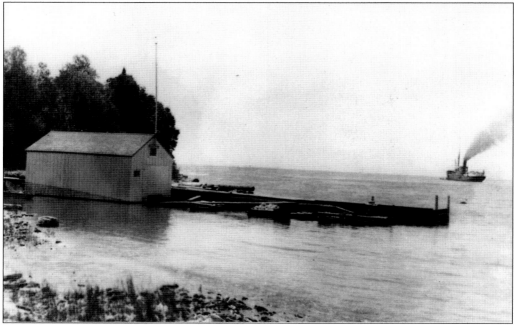

Supplies were brought to lighthouses by Lighthouse Tenders, forerunners of modern Coast Guard buoy tenders. Here the Lighthouse Tender *Dahlia* departs Cana Island after dropping off supplies in July 1913. Supplies were then hauled by wheelbarrow to the light. (Courtesy DCMM & LPS.)

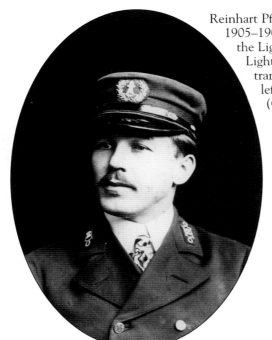

Reinhart Pfiel was first assistant keeper at Cana Island 1905–1909. Born in 1872 in Ellison Bay, he joined the Lighthouse Service in 1902 at Grosse Point Light in Evanston, Illinois. A few years after transferring to Kewaunee Light in 1909, he left the service and returned to Ellison Bay. (Courtesy DCMM & LPS.)

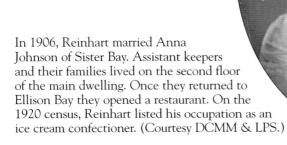

In 1906, Reinhart married Anna Johnson of Sister Bay. Assistant keepers and their families lived on the second floor of the main dwelling. Once they returned to Ellison Bay they opened a restaurant. On the 1920 census, Reinhart listed his occupation as an ice cream confectioner. (Courtesy DCMM & LPS.)

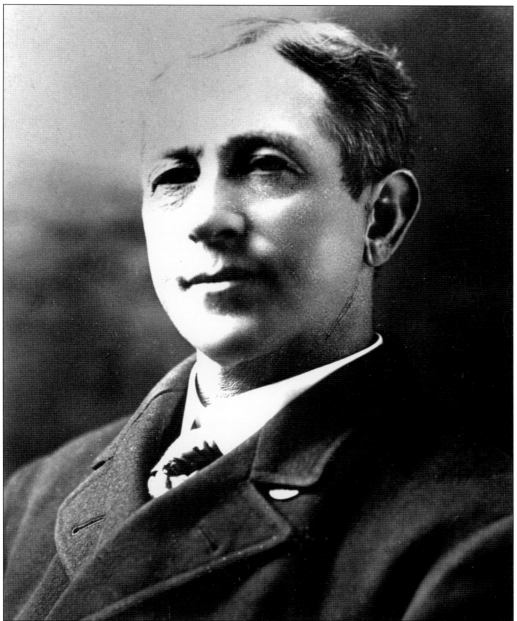

Oscar Knudson (1862–1960) was keeper at Cana Island 1918–1924. On October 2, 1919, he saw the wooden steamer *Frank O'Connor* on fire about two miles off shore. The captain ran the boat aground and the 21-man crew abandoned ship. Knudson and Assistant Picor launched their boat and began towing the lifeboat towards shore. Soon, the Bailey's Harbor Life-Saving crew arrived and took the tow to better care for the survivors. Phone service was installed at the island in 1920 which, along with a car Knudson bought that year, greatly reduced isolation for him and his wife, Maud. He transferred to Grosse Point Light in Evanston, Illinois in 1924 to be close to his son, Ansel, who has just gained admittance to Northwestern University. (Courtesy DCMM & LPS.)

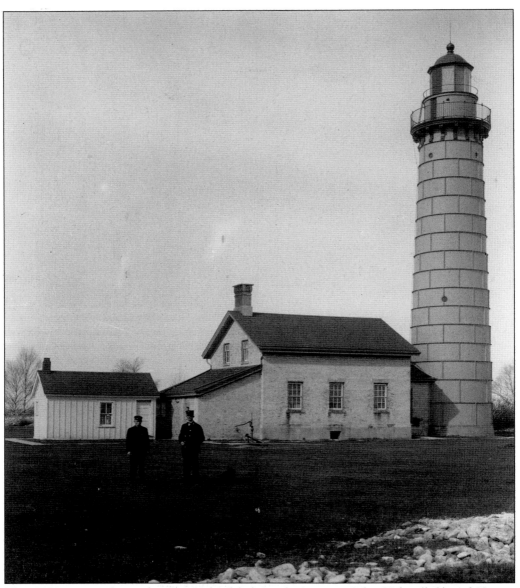

This 1921 images shows the Cana Island light with Assistant John Hahn (left) and Keeper Oscar Knudsen. The structure consists of (from left to right) a summer kitchen built in 1890, a connecting passageway, the original kitchen, the one-and-a-half-story keeper's dwelling, a second connecting passageway, and finally the steel-clad tower, which has an internal circular stairwell. Including their own duties, Cana Island Keepers were tasked with maintaining the unmanned acetylene gas lights in Bailey's Harbor Range (1923) and Eagle Bluff Light (1926). (Courtesy DCMM & LPS.)

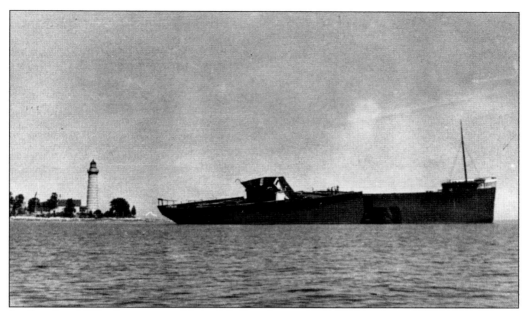

In October 1928, the steamer *Michael J. Bartelme* ran aground in fog on the reef southeast of Cana Island. Built in 1895 as the *John J. McWilliams*, the *Bartelme* was northbound from Milwaukee after delivering a shipment. Keeper Clifford Sanderson phoned the Bailey's Harbor Coast Guard Station crew, who quickly arrived on the scene. (Courtesy DCMM & LPS.)

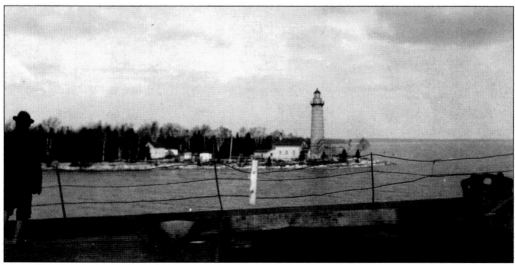

Captain Crockett, the vessel's master, was ordered to start stripping the boat on October 26. On November 10, he made his last trip to the boat and left Cana Island on November 17. He suffered an injury to his foot in the initial grounding, which eventually led to amputation. Everything usable was removed and the *Bartelme* was eventually cut up for scrap. (Courtesy DCMM & LPS.)

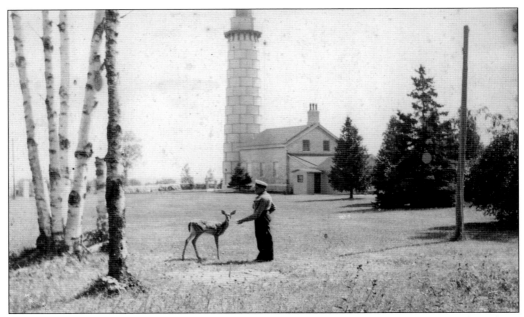

The last civilian keeper was Ross Wright (1932–1941), shown here entertaining a local resident. Wright's 34-year career also included service at Milwaukee, North Manitou, and Manitowoc lights. In 1934, during his tenure, electricity was brought to the island, greatly easing the care of the light. (Courtesy DCMM & LPS.)

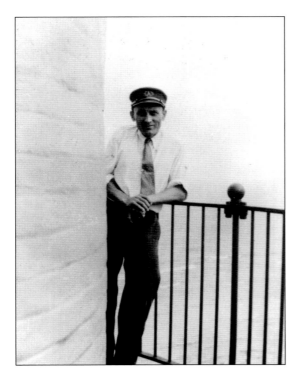

Michael Drezdon was assistant keeper from 1933 to 1941 and then remained under the Coast Guard from 1941 to 1945. Since his departure, the light has been under the full care of Coast Guard personnel who continue to service the active aid to navigation. From 1945 to 1970, the dwelling and land were leased to the McCarthy family. They were leased by the DCMM in the 1970s; the organization continues to operate it as a museum during the summer and fall. (Courtesy DCMM & LPS.)

Five

ISLAND LIGHTS
POTTAWATOMIE, PILOT, PLUM
RANGE, AND CHAMBERS

It is the duty of light-keepers to aid wrecked persons as far as lies in their power.
—Instructions to the Employees of the Lighthouse Service, 1881.

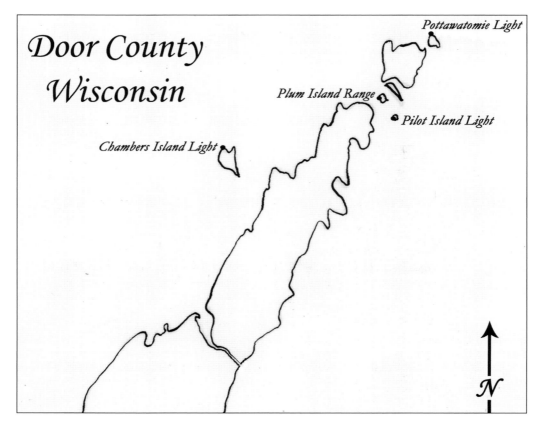

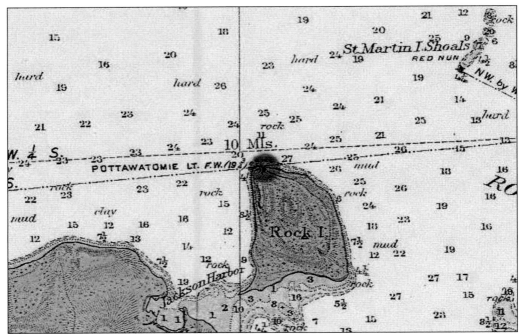

Located at the extreme tip of the peninsula, Pottawatomie Light is perched on Rock Island overlooking Rock Island Pass, a northern entrance into Green Bay, on this 1910 nautical chart. (Courtesy NOAA.)

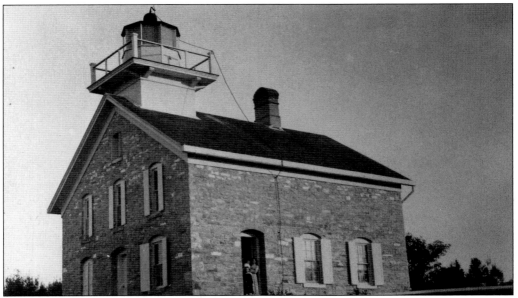

Begun in 1836 and completed in 1837, the original buildings (a tower and separate dwelling) were demolished in 1858 due to poor mortar, and the present Pottawatomie Light was built in their place. The original Winslow Patent light was replaced in 1880 with a 4th order Fresnel lens. In this 1883 photograph, Emily Betts, wife of Keeper William Betts, stands in the doorway with two of their children. (Courtesy NARA.)

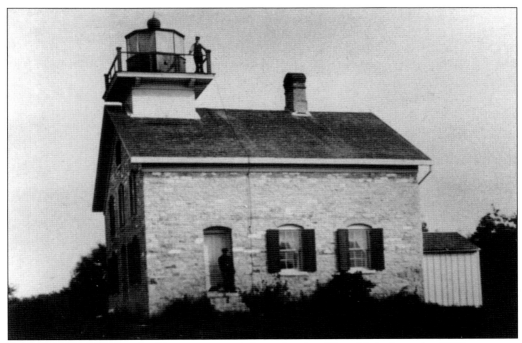

Stone for the two-story building was quarried on the site. The debris from the 1837 structure was thrown over the bluff in 1887 by Keeper Jesse Minor and friend/unofficial assistant Jens Jacobsen. Prior to his death in 1952, Mr. Jacobsen built a history museum, still open to the public, on his Washington Island property. (Courtesy WIA.)

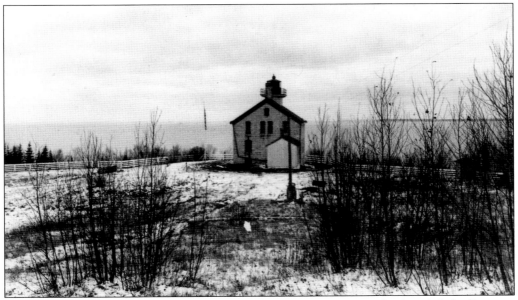

This early 20th-century photograph was taken by George Eastman, who founded the Eastman Kodak Company in 1880. The wooden structure attached at the back of the stone dwelling was a summer kitchen added sometime after 1887. (Courtesy DCMM & LPS.)

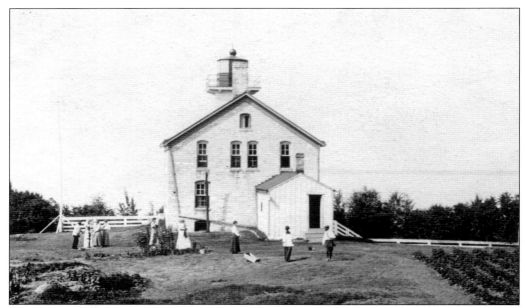

This post-1909 photograph captures what is possibly the large family of Edward Cornell, keeper from 1911 to 1928. The well on the left was finally installed in 1909, after many years of complaints about having to carry lake water up a hundred feet of steps. On the far right are rows of crops grown for use by the family. (Courtesy WIA.)

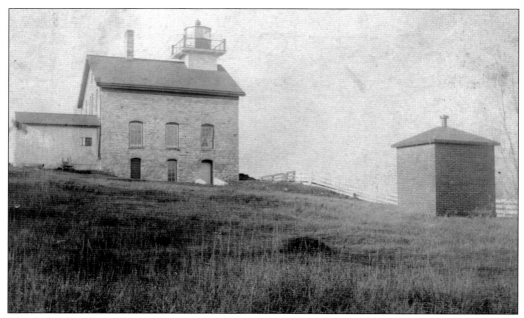

The light first burned sperm oil and was changed to lard oil in 1866 when sperm oil became scarce. Lard oil was laborious as it smoked and would congeal at cooler temperatures. In 1880, the light was converted to kerosene which was easier to use as well as more flammable. The brick oil house on the right was built in 1904 to store the ignitable substance. (Courtesy WIA.)

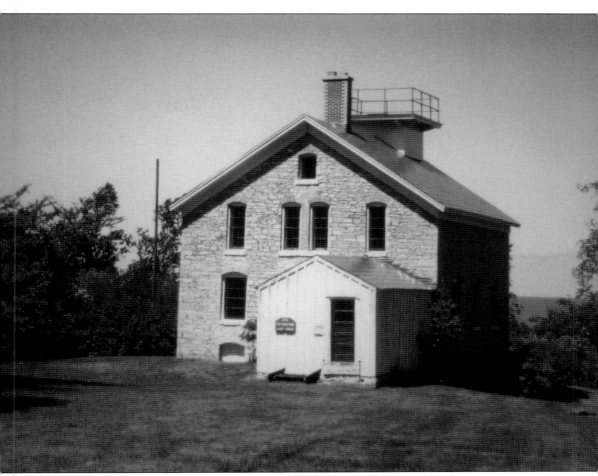

Electricity was never brought to Pottawatomie Light, but it was automated with a battery powered beacon in the mid-1940s. It is thought the original 4th order Fresnel lens was stolen from the lighthouse's basement. In 1986, the Coast Guard installed solar panels to power the light. A few years later, the current skeleton steel tower was built to the west, and the beacon was moved from the stone structure. The lantern room was removed and the tower was capped at that time to reduce damage to the building. The entire structure was restored by the Friends of Rock Island in 2004, including the addition of a reconstructed lantern room in 1999. (Courtesy DCMM & LPS.)

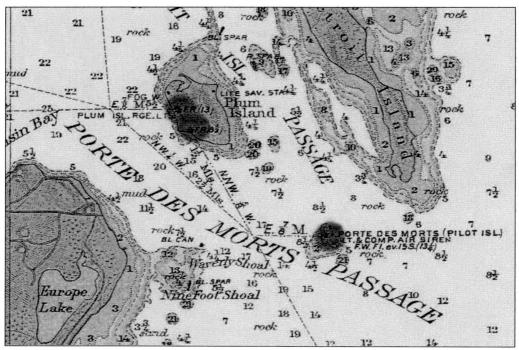

This 1910 nautical chart shows the dangerous Porte Des Morts Passage between the peninsula and Washington Island. There are lights on Pilot Island, originally called "Porte Des Morts Island," on the lower right and on Plum Island in the upper left. (Courtesy NOAA.)

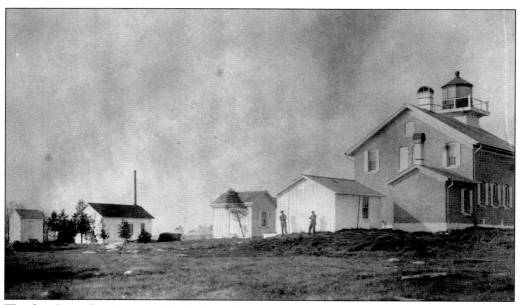

The first Porte Des Morts Light (Pilot Light) was actually built on Plum Island in the 1840s. It was deemed unsuitable to guide mariners and abandoned when the new light was built on Pilot Island in 1858. This 1883 photograph shows the building before additions were made in 1901. (Courtesy USCG.)

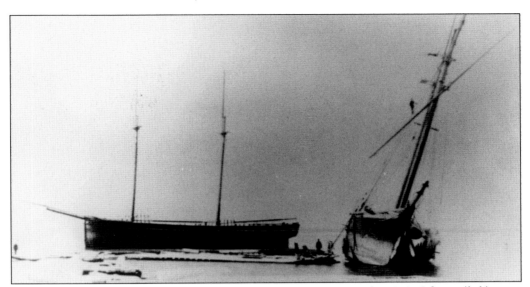

In October 1892, two schooners grounded on the island. The 138-foot *J.E. Gilmore* (left) came ashore on the 17th, while the 147-foot *A.P. Nichols* (right) followed 11 days later. The awash deck of the wreck *Forest* from a year earlier lies between them. Keeper Martin Knudsen received national attention for his daring assistance to the crew of the *Nichols*. He waded out on slippery rocks, grabbed one man who was almost washed away, and led all of them to safety. Three Knudsen brothers (Martin, Peter, and Nelson) would eventually serve as Pilot Island Keepers. (Courtesy DCMM & LPS.)

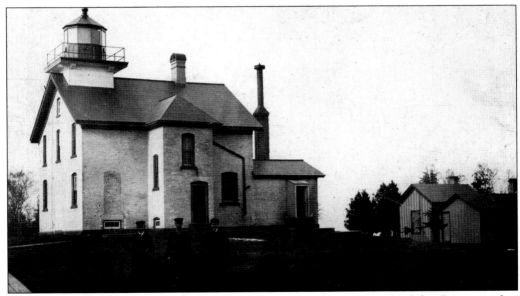

Two assistant keepers met their end while at Pilot Island. In June 1880, John Boyce—either out of isolation and loneliness or despondency from a love affair—cut his own throat. Peter Peterson drowned in December 1898 when the station boat was capsized on the way to Detroit Harbor. This post-1901 picture shows three unidentified keepers and the additions to the main structure. (Courtesy DCMM & LPS.)

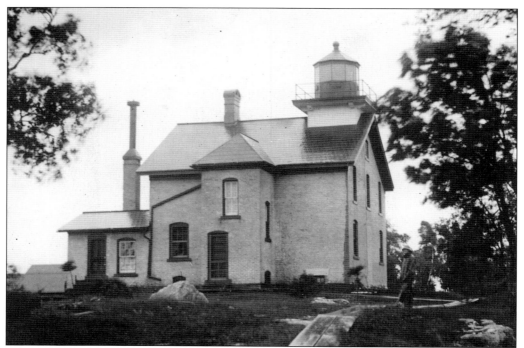

The 4th order Fresnel lens first displayed a flashing white light that was changed to fixed red in 1891. In 1894, the light was changed to a white light that flashed every 15 seconds. The figure in foul weather gear on the right may be Walter Otteson, who was keeper from 1913 to 1923. (Courtesy USCG.)

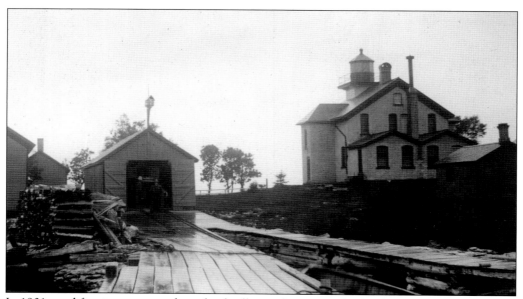

In 1901, modifications were made to the dwelling to better suit the families of the keeper and first assistant. This 1914 photograph shows the side addition which juts out on both sides and allowed separate entrances. Another kitchen was also added onto the back. (Courtesy USCG.)

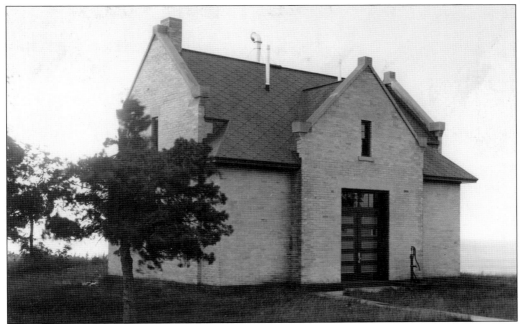

A fog signal was first installed at the light in 1864. The steam whistle was changed to a steam siren in 1875, with a backup siren added in 1880. The brick fog-signal building above was built in 1904 and housed a diesel powered air diaphone. This photograph was taken in July 1913. (Courtesy USCG.)

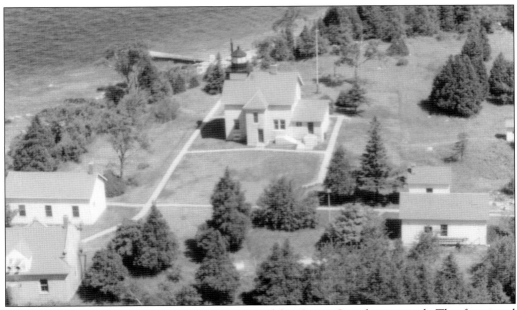

Between 1945 to 1962, the station was manned by Coast Guard personnel. The fog signal was discontinued and the Fresnel lens was removed. The light was automated and powered by batteries and solar cells. This aerial view taken in July 1947 shows the main dwelling, out buildings, and fog signal with horns on the lower left. (Courtesy USCG.)

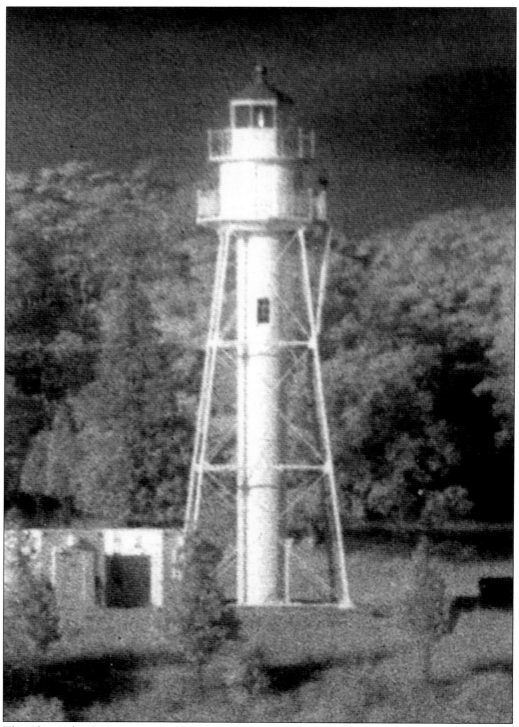

The Plum Island Range was built in 1896 to further help vessels navigating the treacherous shoals and islands in Death's Door Passage. (Courtesy DCMM & LPS.)

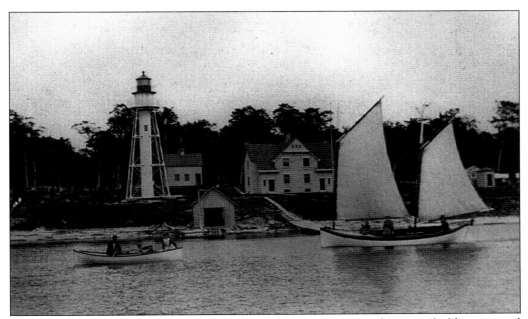

The 65-foot-tall rear range consisted of a skeleton iron frame with a core holding a spiral staircase which ascended to the black cast iron lantern room. The rear range and keeper's buildings are pictured here from the water, c. 1899–1905. (Courtesy USCG.)

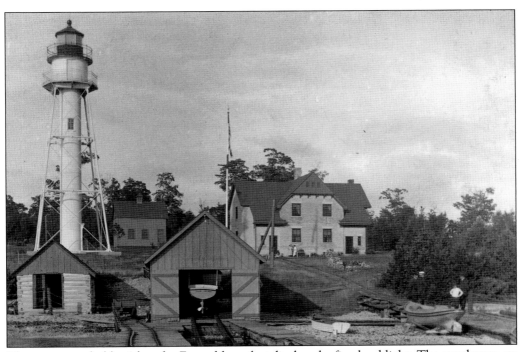

The rear range held a 4th order Fresnel lens that displayed a fixed red light. The gentlemen on the right in this July 1913 picture may be Keeper Charles Boshka and Assistants George Merugs and George Haas. (Courtesy USCG.)

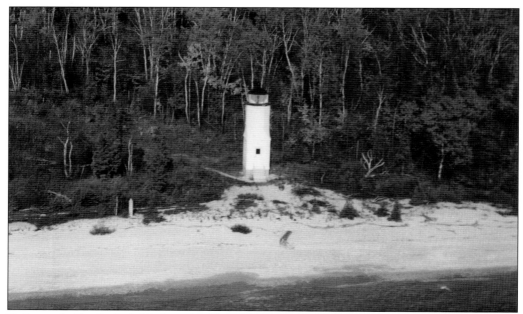

Built much like Bailey's Harbor, the Plum Island Front Range light was a white wooden two-story structure square at the base and octagonal above. A 6th order Fresnel lens in the lantern room displayed a fixed red light. This photograph was taken c. 1947. (Courtesy USCG.)

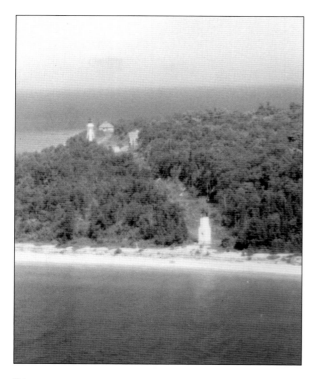

Both Plum Island Range Lights are visible in this July 1947 photograph. They are around 1650 feet apart and were first lit in May 1897. In 1964, the deteriorated wood front range light was replaced with a steel skeletal tower and beacon. (Courtesy USCG.)

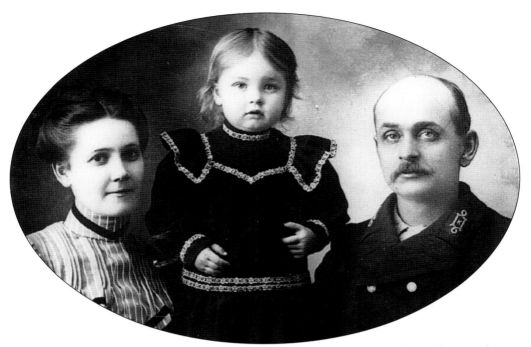

Anna Lind (left), Harriet (center), and Hans Jacob Hanson are pictured here. Hans was keeper of Plum Island from 1899 to 1905 and assistant keeper of Pilot Island from 1897 to1899. He transferred to Menominee North Pier Light as keeper in 1905; he served there until his death while on duty in 1923. (Courtesy DCMM & LPS.)

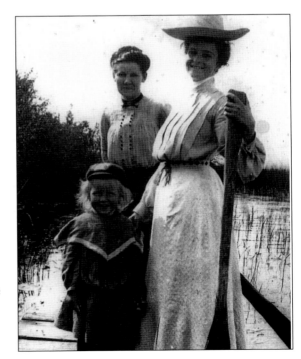

Pictured here, from left to right, are Harriet Hanson, Anna Lind Hanson, and an unidentified woman (possibly the wife of either John Young or George Cornell, assistant keepers). Families were allowed to live on the island and enjoyed helping with maintenance and gardening. (Courtesy DCMM & LPS.)

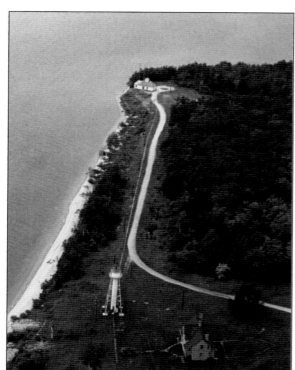

This aerial view taken in July 1947 shows the rear range, the keeper's dwelling in the foreground, and the fog signal building in the distance. The one-story brick fog signal building was in operation from 1897 to 1975. As with other Door County lights, these were eventually electrified and automated. When the Plum Island Coast Guard Station transferred to nearby Washington Island in 1990, the structures on Plum Island were left to the elements, although the lights are still maintained as active aids to navigation. (Courtesy USCG.)

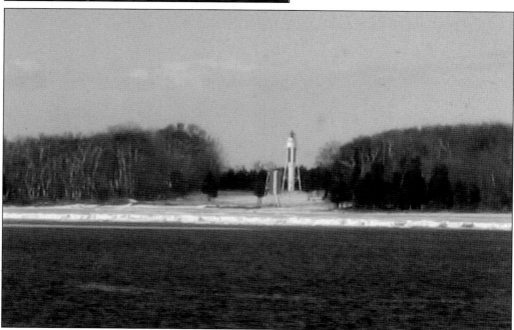

The new steel skeletal front range is visible in this 2005 photograph. Striped day boards have been added to assist the mariner during daylight. There is a current effort to transfer the island and buildings to the Green Bay National Wildlife Refuge for protection and possible restoration. (Authors' Collection.)

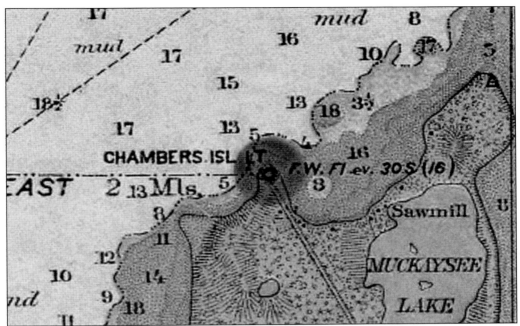

Located in the middle of Green Bay, the approximately 3500-acre Chambers Island was named for Colonel Chambers, who was part of an American expedition on their way to Fort Howard (Green Bay) in 1816. The light is shown on the northwestern peninsula on this 1910 nautical chart. (Courtesy NOAA.)

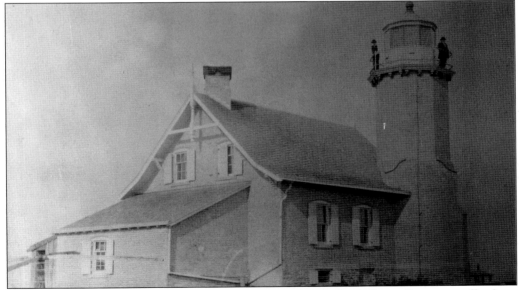

Chambers Island Light was built in 1868 to help guide vessels in Green Bay, especially those passing on the west side of the island. It was constructed in a similar manner to the Eagle Bluff Light, but the tower was given an octagonal shape to distinguish it. Taken in 1883, this photograph shows two unidentified gentlemen on the tower, one of which may be the first keeper, Lewis Williams. (Courtesy NARA.)

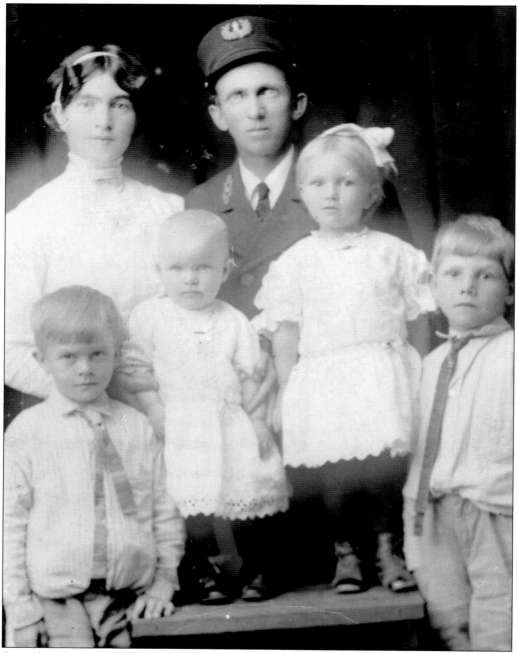

Samuel and Mary Hanson are pictured here in 1913 with their children, from left to right, Edgar, Doris, Sadie, and Clifford. Samuel was first assistant from 1909 to 1923 at Chambers Island. Unfortunately, tragedy repeatedly struck his family during this time. In 1914, Mary unexpectedly died, and in 1921, Edgar died of a ruptured appendix. The next year, Clifford fell through the ice and drowned on the way to Fish Creek for the mail. Samuel transferred to Cana Island as first assistant for six months in 1923, then left the service, only to return in 1925 for two years in Ludington. He passed away in 1942. (Courtesy DCMM & LPS.)

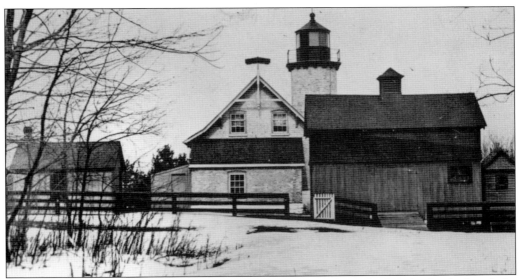

The almost 45-foot-tall tower held a 4th order Fresnel lens which displayed a fixed white light that flashed every 60 seconds. In 1892, the light's characteristics were changed to flash every 30 seconds. The light is shown in this 1914 picture. (Courtesy DCMM & LPS.)

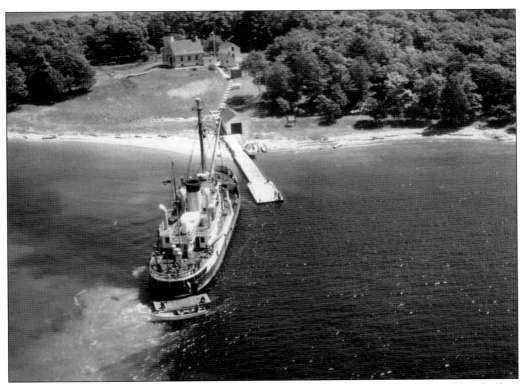

This unidentified tender maneuvers at the Chamber Island Light's pier, c. 1940s. The shallow area is evident in the sand agitated by the vessel's propeller. The large boathouse on shore was built in 1906. (Courtesy USCG.)

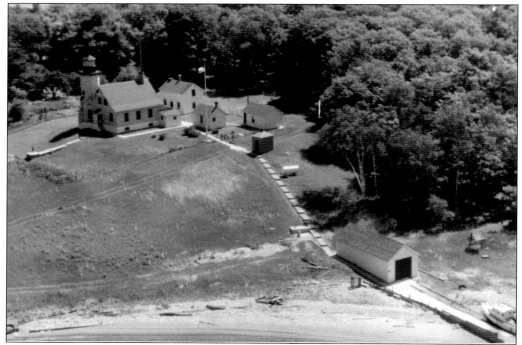

This aerial photograph taken in July 1947 shows the structure before the lantern room was removed in the 1950s and a skeleton frame was erected in its place atop the tower. Some sources state the 4th order Fresnel lens eventually made its way to a museum in Nebraska, while others dispute that claim. (Courtesy USCG.)

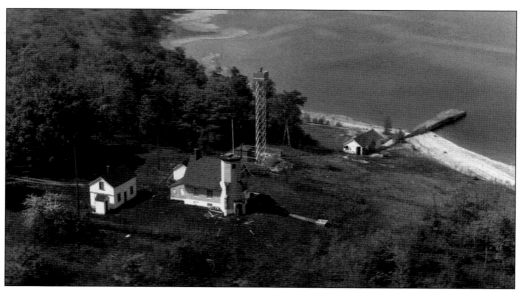

In 1961, the Coast Guard erected a separate steel tower with a beacon as shown in this June 1963 aerial photograph. The missing lantern room is clearly visible. In 1976, the Coast Guard deeded the land and buildings to the Town of Gibraltar for park purposes. Joel and Mary Blahnik are the current caretakers and are working to restore the buildings. (Courtesy USCG.)

Six

LIFE-SAVING STATIONS
STURGEON BAY CANAL, BAILEY'S HARBOR, AND PLUM ISLAND

The Blue Book says we've got to go out and it doesn't say a damn thing about having to come back.
> —Keeper Patrick Etheridge, Cape Hatteras
> Life-Saving Station, North Carolina

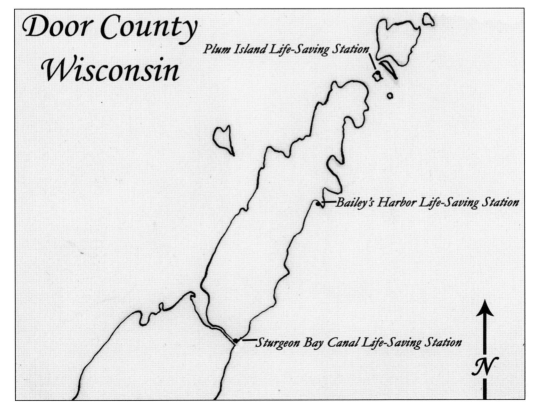

Sturgeon Bay Canal Life-Saving Station

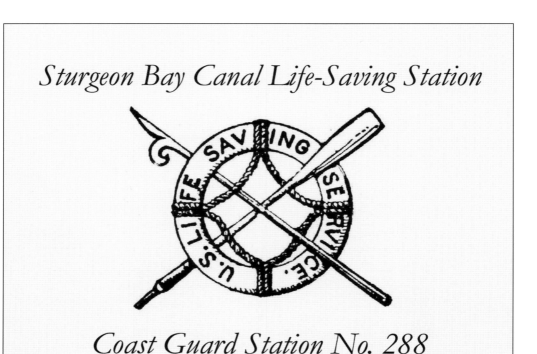

Coast Guard Station No. 288

The Sturgeon Bay Canal Life-Saving Station was designed by Albert Bibb, the U.S. Life-Saving Service Architect, and built in 1886 on the Lake Michigan end of the Sturgeon Bay Ship Canal. Built for $4,560, the station was known as a Bibb #3-type, characterized by a one-and-a-half-story, "L"-shaped building with a double boat bay, lookout cupola, and a walkway running the length of the roof peak. (Courtesy DCMM & LPS.)

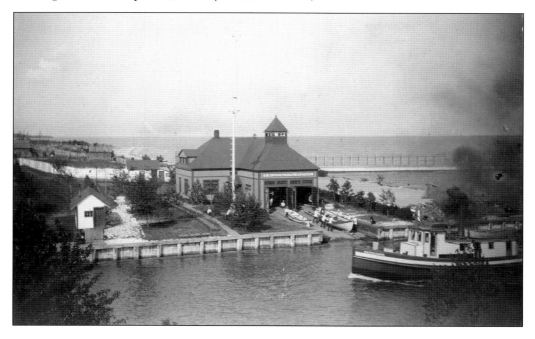

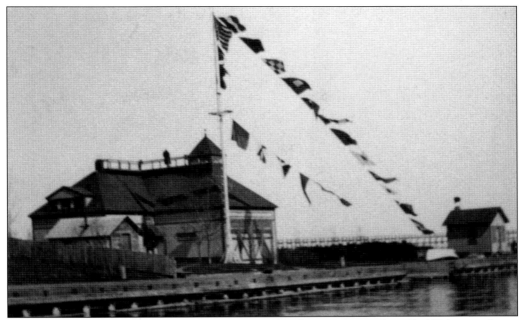

William Nequette was appointed as the station's first keeper. September 15, 1886 opened as a clear day, with a light southwest wind and low surf. This inaugural crew consisted of: McMullen, Oasby, Bauery, Anderson, Dionne, Boutin, and Pilon. Three of these surfman, Joseph Dionne, Telesfford Boutin, and Carl Anderson, following the service's desire to promote from within, later became keepers of the Sturgeon Bay Life-Saving Station. (Courtesy DCMM & LPS.)

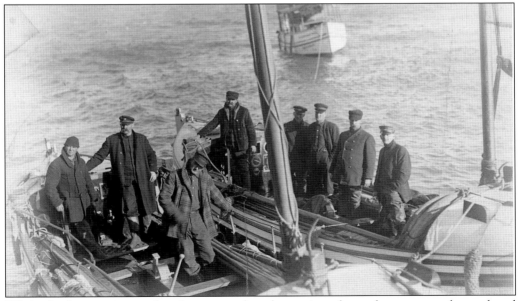

While the keeper was employed year-round at the station, the surfman were only employed during the navigable season, April to December. Most surfman found whatever odd jobs they could to get them through the winter. This is an undated picture of the Sturgeon Bay and Kewaunee crews. (Courtesy DCMM & LPS.)

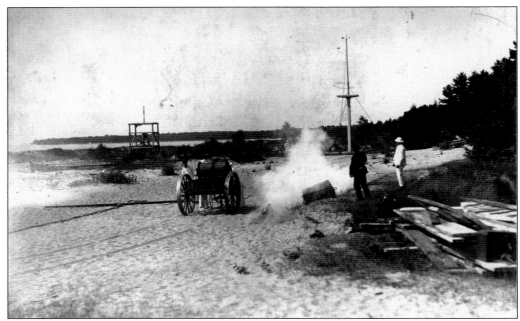

Beach apparatus drills were an important part of life for life-saving station crews. The Lyle Gun, a type of line throwing cannon, is used here to fire a shot line to a wreck pole, a post set in the ground to simulate the spar of a wrecked vessel. It was usually the keeper's responsibility to aim and fire the gun, as high accuracy was required. (Courtesy DCMM & LPS.)

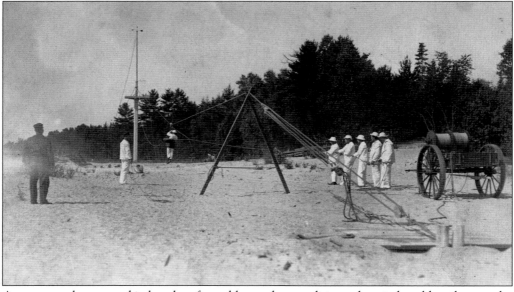

As most wrecks occurred in less than favorable weather conditions, the wind could easily carry the projectile and shot line away from its intended target. If the keeper made his target, the shot line was used to pull heavier lines over to be secured to the mast of the disabled vessel. Once this was accomplished, personnel could be transferred from the imperiled vessel to the safety of shore using a breeches buoy, a life ring with trousers sewn into the middle. (Courtesy DCMM & LPS.)

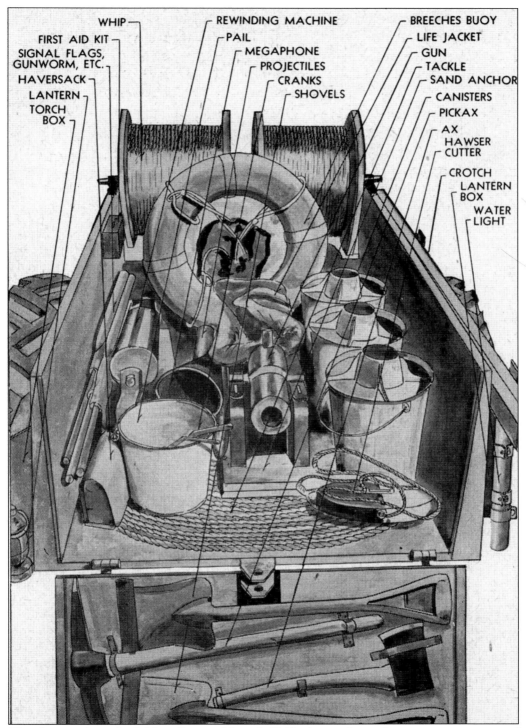

WHIP — REWINDING MACHINE — BREECHES BUOY
FIRST AID KIT — PAIL — LIFE JACKET
SIGNAL FLAGS, — MEGAPHONE — GUN
GUNWORM, ETC. — PROJECTILES — TACKLE
HAVERSACK — CRANKS — SAND ANCHOR
LANTERN — SHOVELS — CANISTERS
TORCH — PICKAX
BOX — AX
HAWSER
CUTTER
CROTCH
LANTERN
BOX
WATER
LIGHT

This drawing from the *Lifeboat Stations Manual*, 1949 edition, shows the numerous contents of the beach apparatus cart. (Courtesy USCG.)

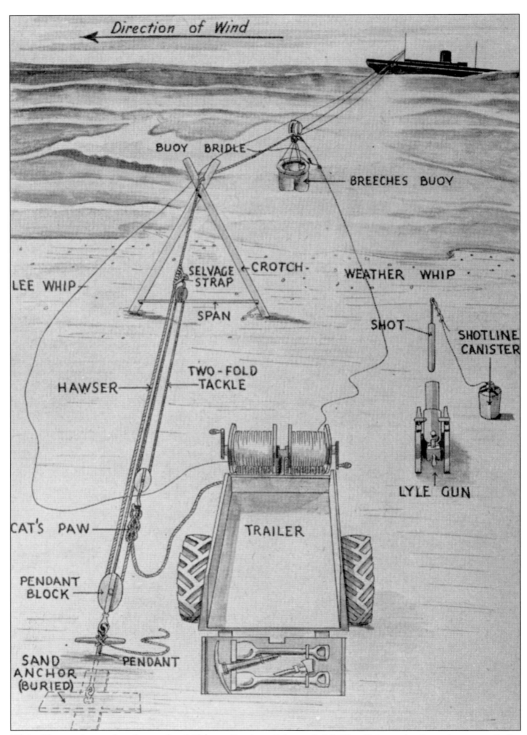

This illustration, also from the *Lifeboat Stations Manual*, 1949 edition, depicts the use of the breeches buoy. (Courtesy USCG.)

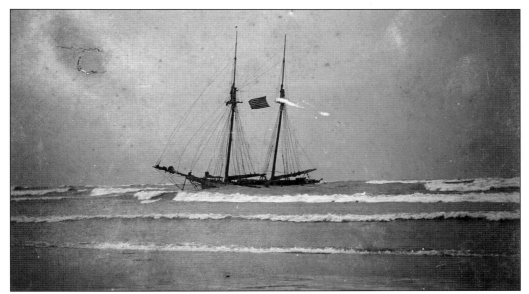

A notable rescue requiring the use of the beach apparatus occurred on October 10, 1895, when the schooner *Otter*, a two master of 205 gross tons, went aground in Whitefish Bay. Built in 1863, the *Otter* had taken on a load of cordwood the previous day and anchored for the night. A raging storm approached, the anchor line parted, and they were soon driven aground. (Courtesy DCMM & LPS.)

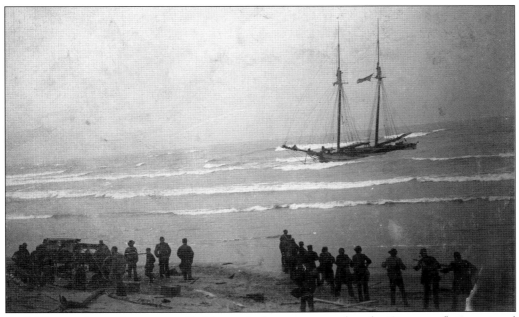

At 9:10 a.m., the station was notified by a telephone message that the *Otter* was flying a signal of distress and was aground one-quarter mile from shore. The life-savers loaded their surfboat and beach apparatus onto a dump scow to transport them four miles to town. From Sturgeon Bay, the life-savers and their equipment were transported eight miles north by horse and wagon. (Courtesy DCMM & LPS.)

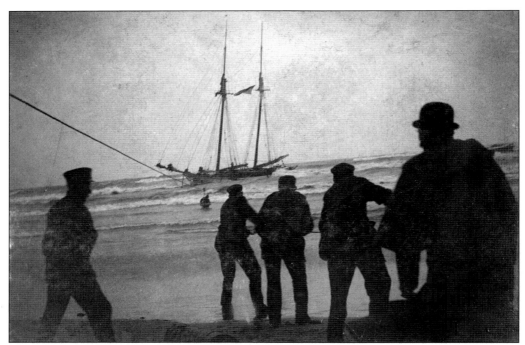

Arriving at Whitefish Bay at 11:30 a.m., the surfmen promptly set up their beach apparatus and landed a successful shot with the Lyle gun. In this photograph, the *Otter*'s Captain Kaufman is brought ashore in the breeches buoy. (Courtesy DCMM & LPS.)

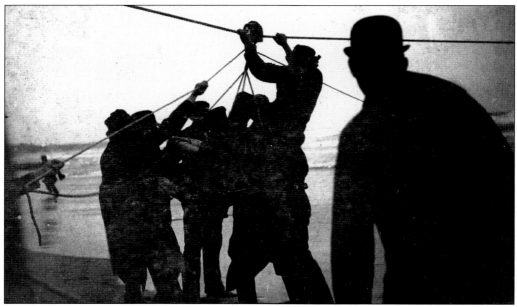

Shortly after the six men were safely brought ashore, the schooner went to pieces and was a total loss. These spectacular images were captured by William A. Drumb, a photographer and journalist who later moved to Wisconsin Dells and established a newspaper which remains in circulation today. (Courtesy DCMM & LPS.)

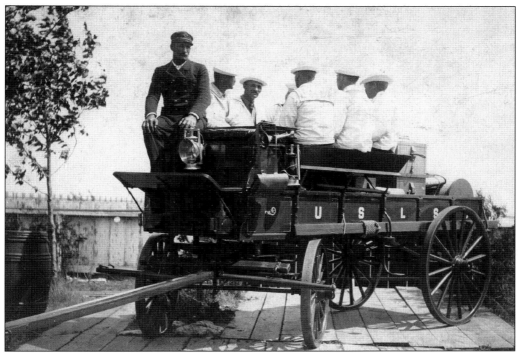

After the *Otter* rescue, Keeper Carl Anderson and his surfman pose for Mr. Drumb atop their beach apparatus wagon. (Courtesy DCMM & LPS.)

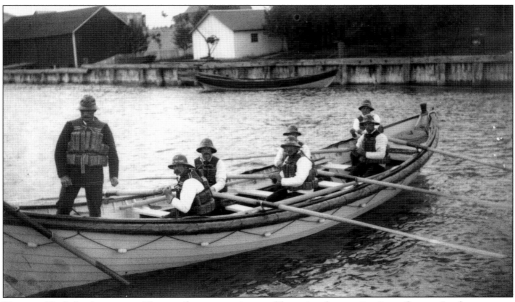

Keeper Carl Anderson and his surfman are pictured here in the station's surfboat. Anderson was the fourth keeper of the Canal Station, and was one of the original surfmen when the station opened in 1886. Notice the cork life vests which were standard flotation at the time. (Courtesy DCMM & LPS.)

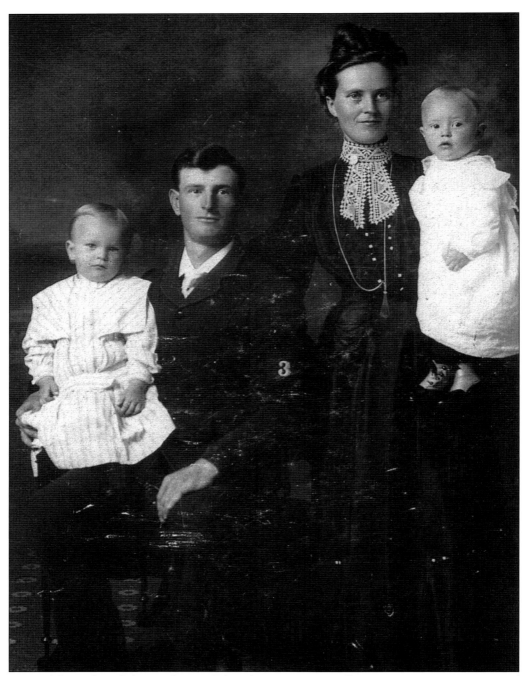

Pictured here, from left to right, are Edward Montgomery, Albert Foster, Lorenza Baury, and Gerald Louis Brown. The photograph was taken in 1904 when Albert was the No. 3 Surfman at the Sturgeon Bay Canal Life-Saving Station. Eventually, all eight Brown children would be born at the station. Albert's father, Jesse Thomas Brown, was keeper at Cana Island from 1891 to 1913. He wrote in Cana Island's log when he left that station to attend their wedding in 1901. (Courtesy DCMM & LPS.)

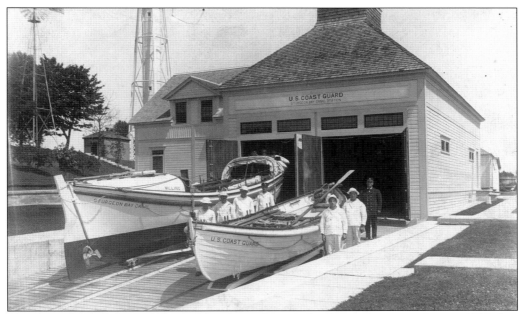

This next series of photographs outlines the surfboat drills; the images were taken in 1919, four years after the Life-Saving Service merged with the Revenue Cutter Service to form the U.S. Coast Guard. This photograph shows the crew standing by the surfboat for inspection. The larger vessel to the left is the station's 34-foot motor lifeboat named *Willing*. (Courtesy DCMM & LPS.)

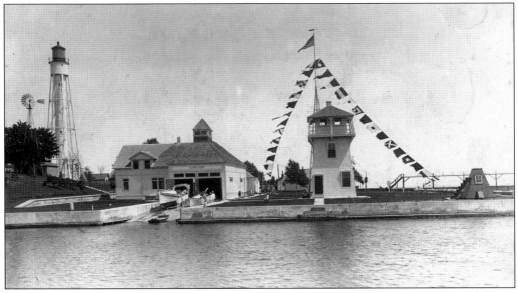

The daily routine was set by the service and was the same for every station. Monday was set aside for the maintenance of the boats and beach apparatus, Tuesday was for drilling in the boats, Wednesday required signaling training, Thursday was for drilling with the beach apparatus, on Friday the crew practiced the "method for restoring the apparently drowned," and Saturday was reserved for housekeeping. (Courtesy DCMM & LPS.)

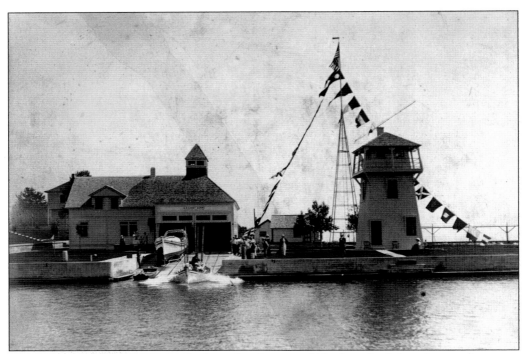

Many Great Lakes stations were built so that boats could be launched directly into the water. (Courtesy DCMM & LPS.)

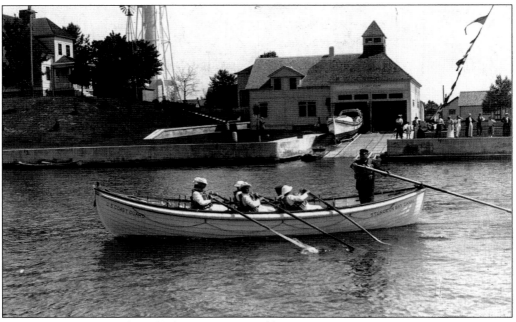

Once a surfboat was launched, the crew would practice rowing to maintain proficiency. Regulations required that each surfboat drill involve at least 30 minutes of rowing. (Courtesy DCMM & LPS.)

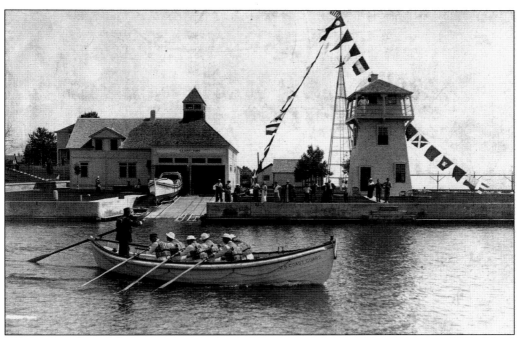

The keeper manned the steering oar at the stern to control the direction of the vessel. The No. 1 Surfman would also cross-train in this position in case anything should ever happen to the keeper during a rescue. (Courtesy DCMM & LPS.)

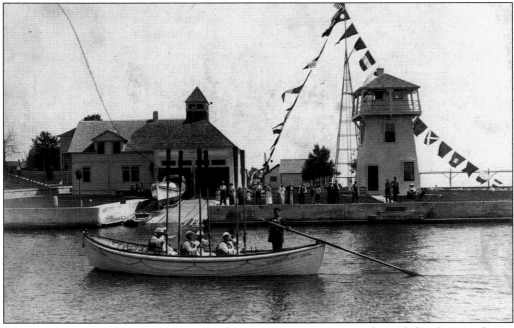

The crew prepares for the capsize test. As this maneuver was very popular with locals, an audience could normally be found at any station conducting such drills. (Courtesy DCMM & LPS.)

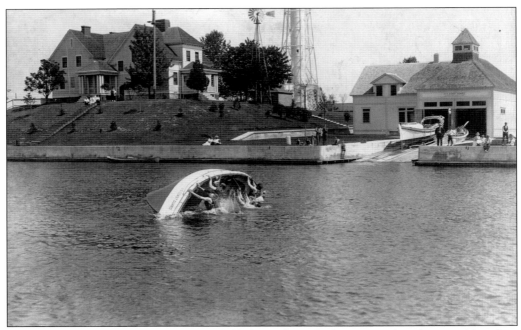

Some surfmen and keepers became so skilled at rolling the boat over that they would end up on top of the capsized hull hardly wet. (Courtesy DCMM & LPS.)

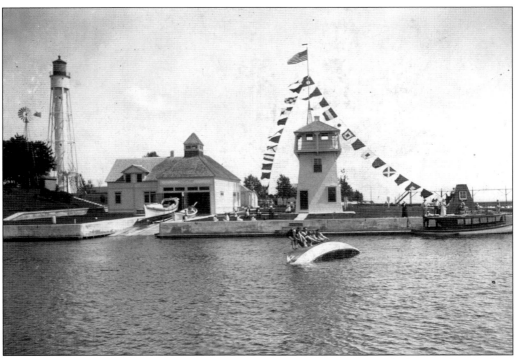

After the boat was rolled, it would be righted by the crew standing on the hull and using their weight to flip it over. (Courtesy DCMM & LPS.)

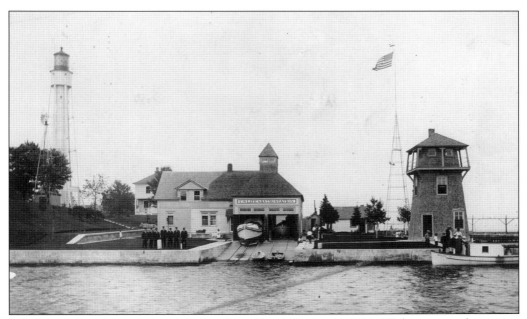

Life-Saving Service crew pose in front of the Canal Station in 1914. Within a year, the station and crew would be part of the newly formed U.S. Coast Guard. Note the additions to the station since its construction in 1886. (Courtesy DCMM & LPS.)

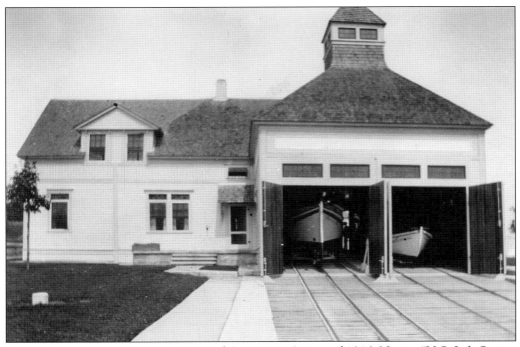

Pictured here is the Sturgeon Bay Canal Station in August of 1916. Notice "U.S. Life Saving Station" had been removed from above the boathouse doors; "U.S. Coast Guard" had yet to be added. (Courtesy USCG.)

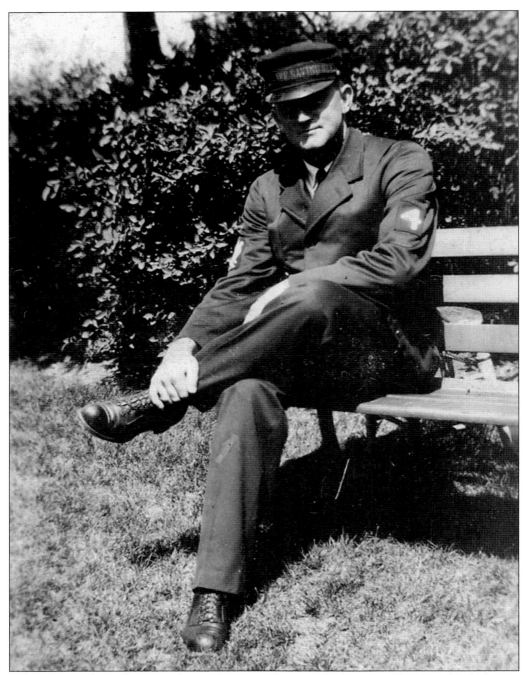

Rube Hitt, is shown here, *c.* 1914, as No. 4 surfman at the Sturgeon Bay Canal Life-Saving Station. He would eventually serve a total of six years in the service. He then became one of the original bridge tenders for the Michigan Street bridge in Sturgeon Bay, a position he held from 1931 to 1957. He passed away at age 77 in 1965, but many Hitt family members still remain in Door County. His son, George Hitt, donated the excellent surfboat drill photographs to the DCMM & LPS. (Courtesy DCMM & LPS.)

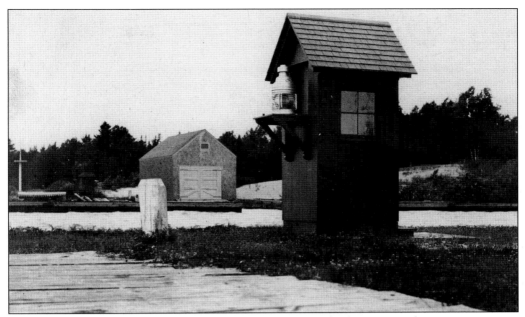

Many Great Lakes stations, including Sturgeon Bay, were built on a canal or river entrance, which posed special problems if a vessel were to encounter trouble on the opposite side. To help correct the problem, Sturgeon Bay Canal Station built a boathouse on the south side of the canal. This south-side boathouse contained an extra surfboat and beach apparatus cart. Also notice the wreck pole on the left for beach apparatus drills. (Courtesy USCG.)

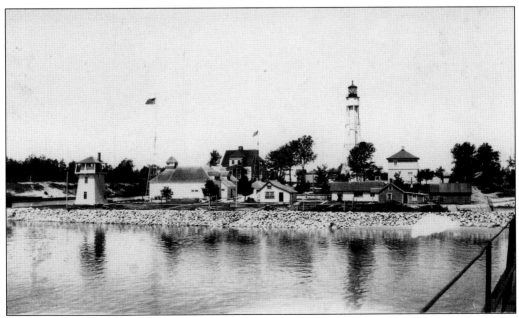

Taken from the Sturgeon North Pierhead Light in 1929–1930, this overall view of the station's grounds show surfmen's cottages in the foreground. Regulations allowed surfmen to build cottages on station grounds at their own expense. (Courtesy DCMM & LPS.)

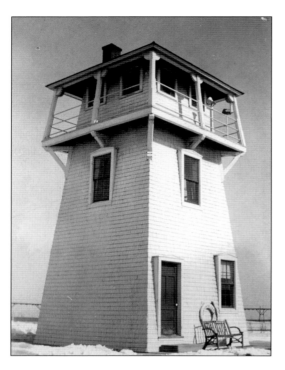

This detached lookout tower was built at the Sturgeon Bay Canal Station in 1904, because the main station with its lookout cupola was built too far back from the lakefront to allow a good view up and down the shore. (Courtesy USCG.)

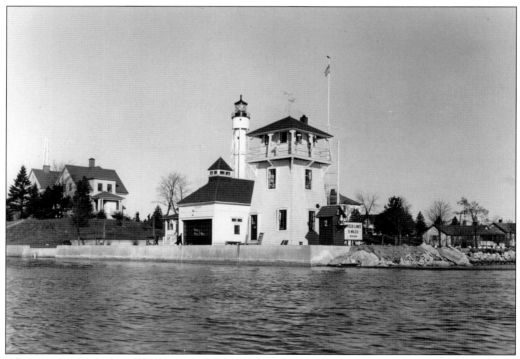

Above we can see the relative position of the detached lookout tower to the main station with its lookout cupola. (Courtesy USCG.)

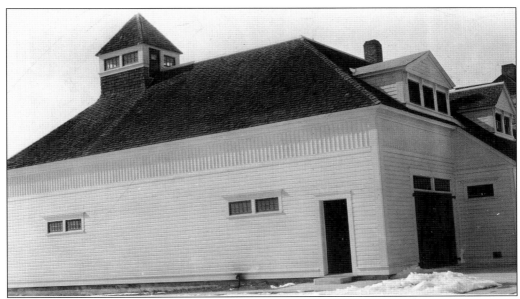

Although unused, the lookout cupola remained atop the main station until 1966. Notice the small door on the backside of the cupola leading to the long-since removed rooftop walkway. (Courtesy USCG.)

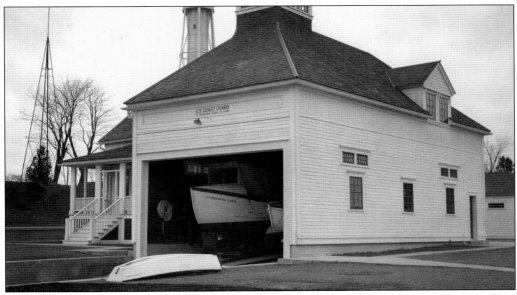

Sometime between 1930 and 1966, the entire station was jacked up several feet to allow clearance for the ever-increasing size of craft used by the U.S. Coast Guard. Compare the side wall of this photograph to the side wall of the photograph above. Pay special attention to the door at the rear of the building in relation to the windows. (Courtesy USCG.)

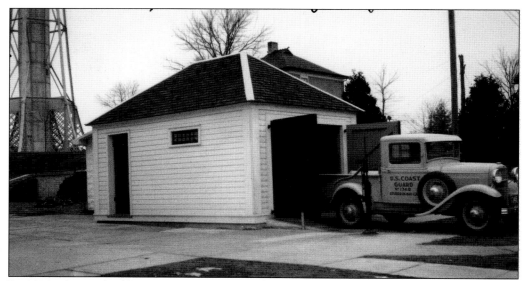

In 1933, this outbuilding was converted to a garage. The U.S. Coast Guard, along with its predecessor, the U.S. Life-Saving Service, has always had to "do more with less." Even today, the frugality of the service is unparalleled. (Courtesy USCG.)

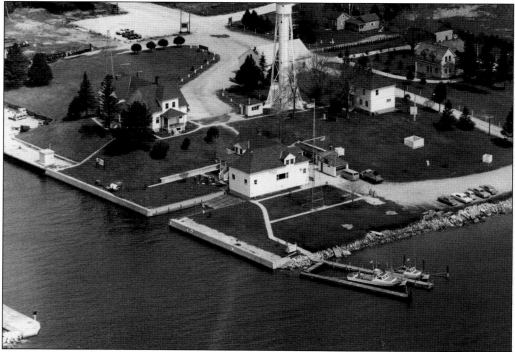

In 1966, the boathouse was enclosed, and the unused lookout cupola was removed as the boats the Coast Guard was now using finally outgrew the boathouse. Also, notice that the detached lookout tower had been removed due to the increasing reliability of radio communications. (Courtesy USCG.)

Bailey's Harbor Life-Saving Station

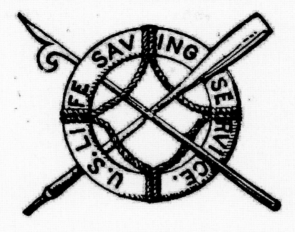

Coast Guard Station No. 289

Prior to the completion of the Sturgeon Bay Ship Canal in 1880, Bailey's Harbor was one of the few harbors of refuge for vessels plying the waters between Milwaukee and Porte Des Morts Passage. As a result, the U.S. Life-Saving Service acquired land in Bailey's Harbor for a station in 1878. Due to a lack of funds and the opening of the canal, however, a station was not built until 1896. (Courtesy DCMM & LPS.)

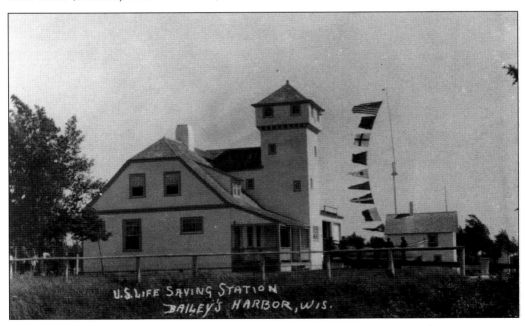

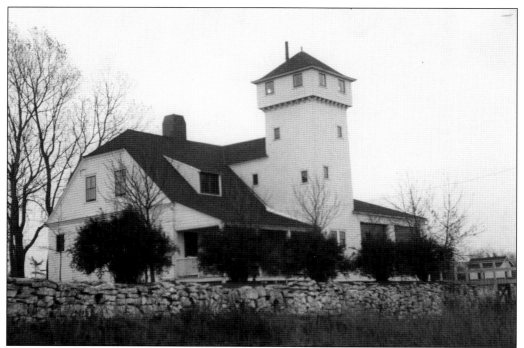

Designed by George Toleman, the one-and-a-half-story building featured double boat-bay doors and a prominent four-story lookout tower. This style was dubbed "Duluth" for the city in which it was first built. The Plum Island Life-Saving Station was built to the same design in the same year. (Courtesy USCG.)

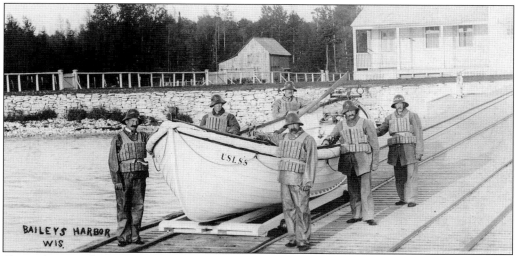

Shown here are First Keeper Peter O. Lavenger, formerly Peter Olsen, and his surfmen. A crew complement of six, including the keeper, was almost the bare minimum to effectively maneuver a surfboat. Like the Sturgeon Bay crew, these men were only hired eight months out of the year and were on their own during the winter months. Once members of the Coast Guard, surfmen were finally hired year-round in 1915 and received a pension upon 30 years of service. (Courtesy DCMM & LPS.)

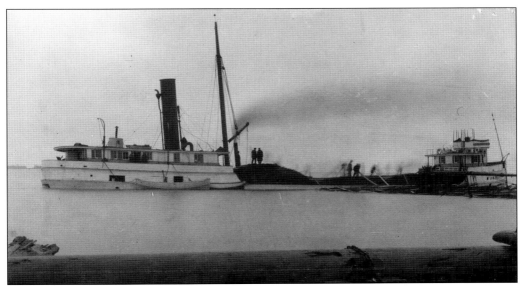

On Oct 27, 1916, the steamer *Philetus Sawyer* was en route to Chicago when heavy leaking forced it into Bailey's Harbor. While at anchor, the steamer's crew frantically tried to keep the boat afloat. The station crew went to help, but their combined efforts could not keep the vessel off the bottom. To make matters worse, a gale blew in, resulting in a few crew injuries. Eventually, the station took 15 crewmembers off the vessel, which was later patched and refloated. (Courtesy DCMM & LPS.)

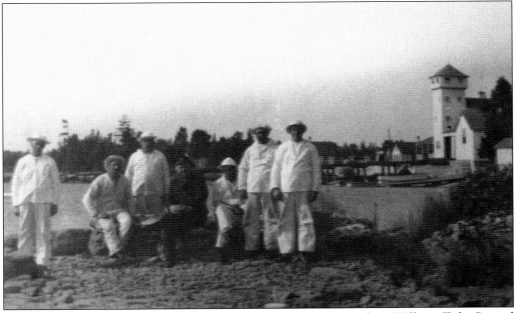

This *c.* 1915 photograph shows, from left to right, Reinhart Hickey, William Toft, Conrad Grovogel, Keeper John Stahl, Raymond Anclam, Jacob Sorenson, and David Jacobson. It is William Toft's family for which Toft Point just north of Bailey's Harbor is named. Both William and his brother, Sam, served in the Life-Saving Service. (Courtesy DCL.)

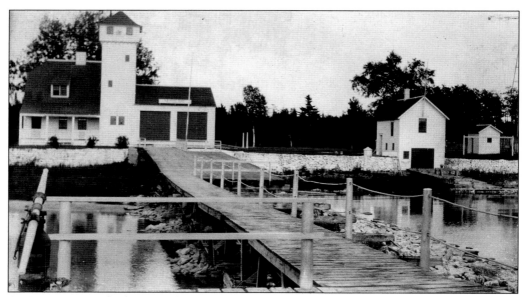

By August 1926, the boats of the service had outgrown the station and a detached boathouse was built. Here we see the walkway out to the boathouse utilizing part of the old launchway. (Courtesy USCG.)

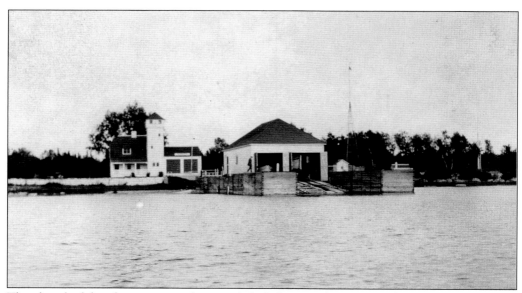

The detached boathouse not only provided shelter to the service's larger boats, but with its offshore extension, it provided access to deeper water in the relatively shallow harbor. (Courtesy USCG.)

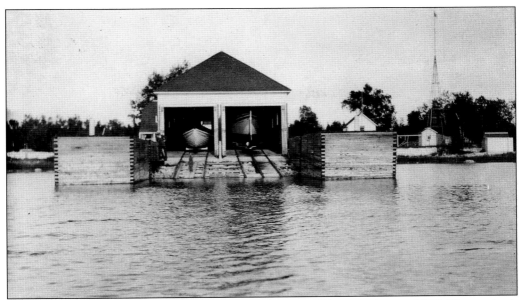

Bailey's Harbor Coast Guard Station boathouse is pictured here in August 1928. The station's surfboat is on the left and the lifeboat is on the right. Notice this lifeboat is lying alongside the *Bartelme* in the picture below. (Courtesy USCG.)

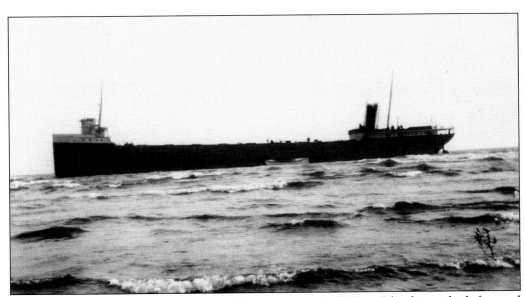

On Oct 11, 1928, the steamer *M.J. Bartelme* ran aground off Cana Island in a thick fog, and the station removed the steamer's 26 men and stood by. With her back broken, the vessel was deemed unsalvageable by underwriters, and she was cut up for scrap. Pieces of the *M.J. Bartelme* still litter the lake floor just a little southeast of Cana Island. Although no lives were lost during the wreck, in 1932 a boy trying to swim to the wreckage was caught in an undertow and drowned. The body was recovered by the Bailey's Harbor crew the following day. (Courtesy DCMM & LPS.)

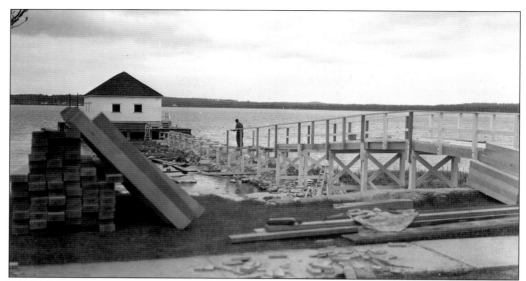

The Bailey's Harbor Station was progressively phased out as the harbor was used less commercially and technological advancements in marine design and safety made more transits occur further from shore. On May 1, 1933, all except two of the surfmen were transferred to other various stations on the lakes. Even with this two man crew, maintenance continued, and in May of 1940, the walkway to the boathouse was replaced. (Courtesy USCG.)

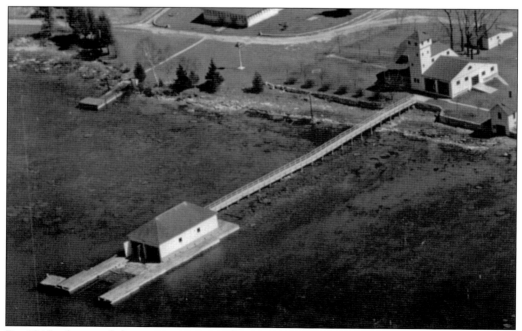

By 1948, the need for a station in Bailey's Harbor had diminished, and the station was abandoned. The responsibility for the waters around Bailey's Harbor was split between the Sturgeon Bay Canal and the Plum Island Stations. George H. Moe was the last full keeper of Bailey's Harbor Station. (Courtesy BHYCR.)

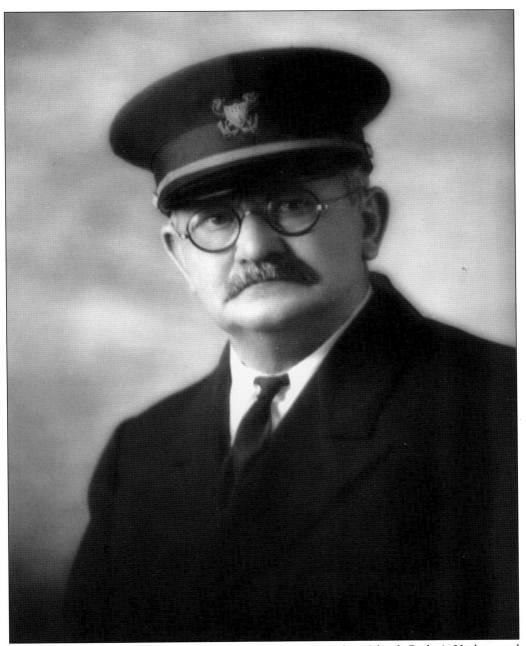

George H. Moe served at all three Door County stations: Plum Island, Bailey's Harbor, and Sturgeon Bay. Having joined the U.S. Life-Saving Service on April 1st, 1898, Moe ended his career as a Boatswain in Kewaunee where he was the Officer in Charge of the station. After nearly 37 years of government service, Moe retired in 1935 at age 64. (Courtesy JHMM.)

Plum Island Life-Saving Station

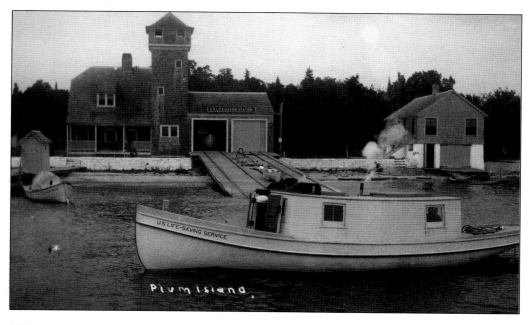

Coast Guard Station No. 290

Prior to the completion of the Ship Canal, all vessels entering Green Bay had to use Death's Door Passage or proceed north around Washington Island through Rock Island Pass. Even with the new canal, larger vessels, those with cumbersome tows, or those en route to Escanaba still had to transit the northern passages. This rocky, treacherous passage was the justification for the Plum Island Life-Saving Station pictured here in 1913. (Courtesy USCG.)

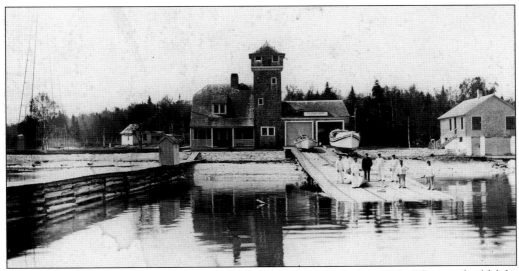

In 1895, a contract for $9,000 was awarded to Marinette contractor C.J. Olson to build life-saving stations at both Plum Island and Bailey's Harbor. Within the year, the Duluth style one-and-a-half-story station characterized by double boat bay doors and a prominent four-story tower was built on the northeast end of the small island. Both stations were drafted by George Toleman and first built in Duluth—thus the name. The Plum Island Station officially opened at noon on August 4, which in an interesting twist of time would eventually be recognized as the anniversary of the Coast Guard, August 4, 1790. (Courtesy DCMM & LPS.)

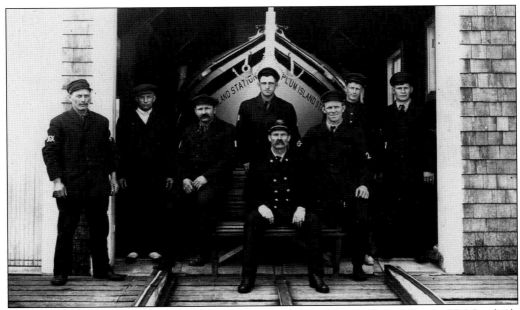

The Plum Island crew is pictured here in 1915. Seated from left to right are George H. Moe (#1), Captain John Christianson (keeper), and Daniel Magnussen (#2). Standing from left to right are Wellington G. Lockhart (#3), Adolph Tostenson (Sub), Richard Johnson (#6), Melvin Peterson (#7), and Mathew Jacobson (#5). Robert Gunnerson (#4) is missing in this photograph. The numbers designate which surfman position they held. (Courtesy DCMM & LPS.)

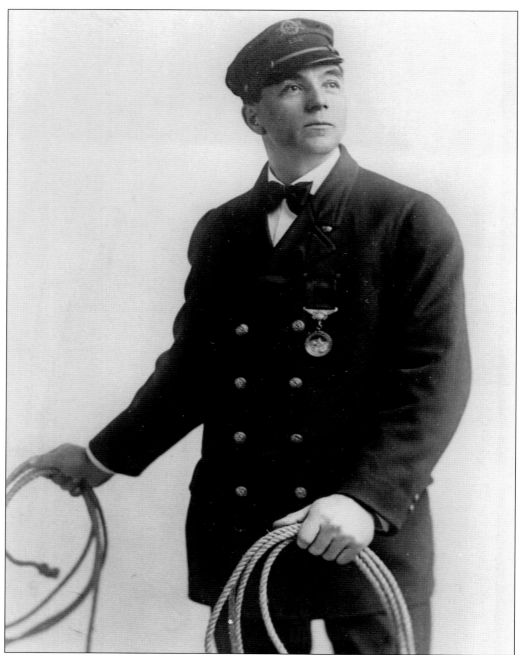

Appointed in February 1896, Keeper Ingar Olsen reported in March to prepare the station for duty. Olsen is shown here wearing the Gold Lifesaving Medal he received for an exceptional rescue while a surfman at the Milwaukee Life-Saving Station in 1893. A 15-man work crew had been trapped by a gale in the air lock of a waterworks crib; all but James Miller perished. After the life-savers arrived and put over a line, Olsen threw himself into the elements and made his way hand over hand. Finding the sole survivor, Olsen tied him to the line and, taking a firm grasp himself, they were pulled to safety. (Courtesy JHMM.)

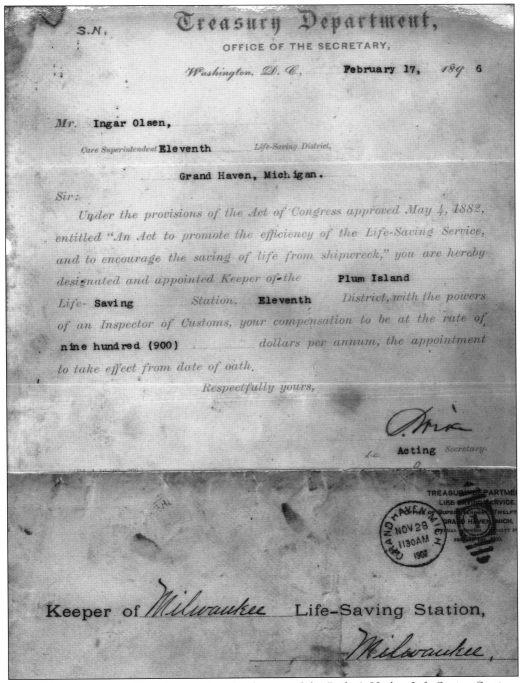

Treasury Department,

OFFICE OF THE SECRETARY,

S.N.

Washington, D. C., **February 17,** *189* 6

Mr. **Ingar Olsen,**

Care Superintendent **Eleventh** *Life-Saving District,*

Grand Haven, Michigan.

Sir :

Under the provisions of the Act of Congress approved May 4, 1882, entitled "An Act to promote the efficiency of the Life-Saving Service, and to encourage the saving of life from shipwreck," you are hereby designated and appointed Keeper of the **Plum Island** Life-**Saving** Station, **Eleventh** District, with the powers of an Inspector of Customs, your compensation to be at the rate of **nine hundred (900)** dollars per annum, the appointment to take effect from date of oath.

Respectfully yours,

Acting *Secretary.*

Keeper of *Milwaukee* Life-Saving Station,

Milwaukee,

Ingar Olsen was originally to be appointed as keeper of the Bailey's Harbor Life-Saving Station, but this was changed to Plum Island Life-Saving Station. No doubt Olsen's heroic Milwaukee rescue had helped him gain his promotion. This document is the appointment letter which gave Olsen command of the new Plum Island Life-Saving Station with the annual salary of $900. He served as keeper until 1901 when he transferred to Milwaukee. (Courtesy DCMM & LPS.)

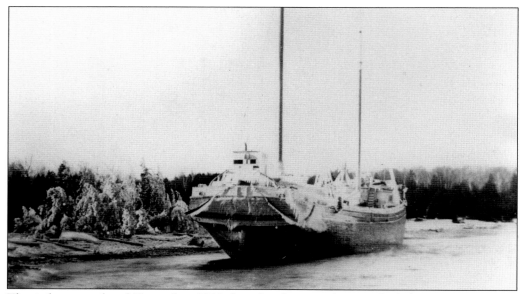

The infamous gale of November 1913 forced a few vessels to seek shelter in Washington Harbor on the northwest corner of Washington Island. In 70-mile-per-hour winds, the station crewmembers carried their beach apparatus first by boat to Detroit Harbor, then over 3 miles of land to the threatened vessels. Originally summoned by the empty steamer, *Louisiana*, the vessel was already on fire on the beach, the first casualty of the great storm. Nearby, the barge *Halsted* (in these two pictures) was also in imminent peril but was too far to get over a line. (Courtesy DCMM & LPS.)

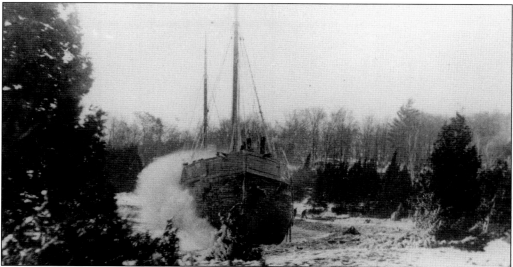

After 20 hours of howling wind and snow, the vessel was finally close enough for a line and breeches buoy to be set up. Right before it was used, however, the barge was astonishingly picked up by a monstrous wave and laid close enough to land that the crew could wade ashore. The life-saving crew continued to stand by for other vessels until the storm abated. By the time the Plum Island crew returned to the station, they had been on duty for over three days in sub-freezing temperatures and whole gale-force winds. (Courtesy DCMM & LPS.)

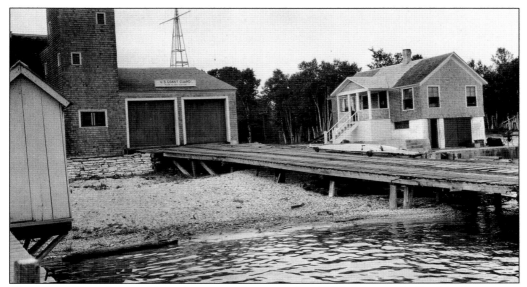

The original boat bay and launch way are shown in this 1927 photograph. By this time, water level and boat size made the old boat bay obsolete. (Courtesy USCG.)

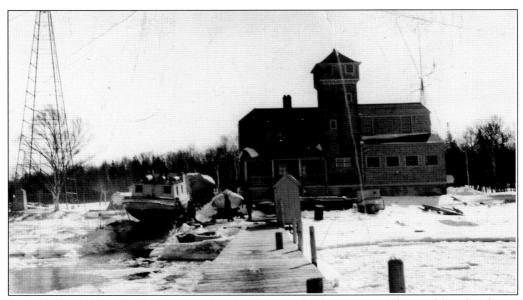

By 1930, the old boat bay had been enclosed and was used as living space. The need for a boathouse is evident as boats hauled out for the winter are exposed to the elements. (Courtesy USCG.)

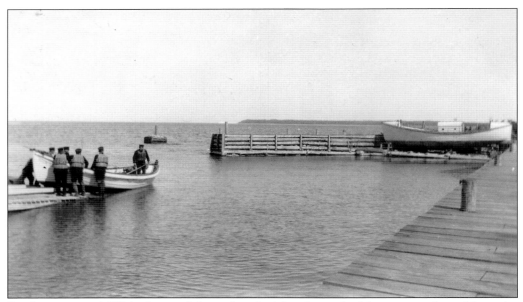

By the winter of 1924, the need for a detached boathouse had become evident. Here, the surfmen are attempting to launch their surfboat which is aground at the end of the ramp. A motor lifeboat is on the right. (Courtesy USCG.)

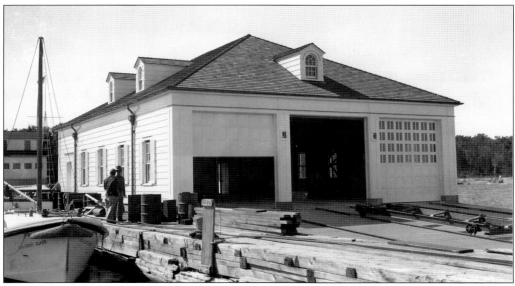

A boathouse was finally built in the 1930s. The large three-bay structure was nearing completion in this 1939 photograph. (Courtesy USCG.)

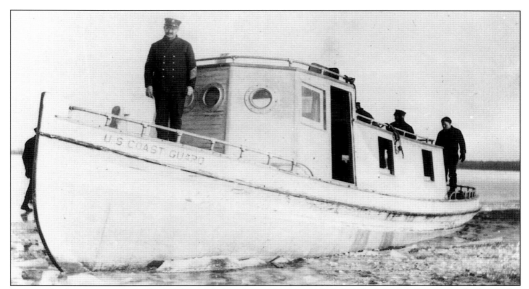

In 1925, the Coast Guard authorized the construction of CG 2613, a 36-foot supply boat for service at Coast Guard Station Plum Island. For her ability to fight through anything, summer or winter, the crew named her *The Bull*. She is now on display at the Jackson Harbor Maritime Museum on Washington Island. (Courtesy DCMM & LPS.)

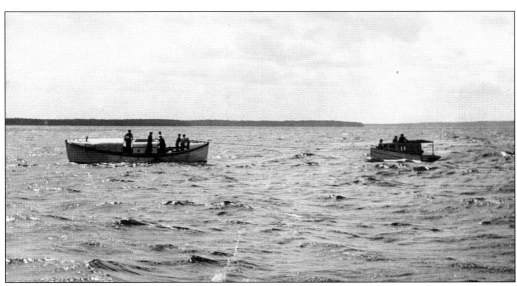

A Coast Guard 36-foot motor lifeboat from Station Plum Island tows a disabled pleasure craft through Death's Door Passage. Providing assistance to pleasure craft became an increasing responsibility as recreational boating increased in the 20th century. (Courtesy DCMM & LPS.)

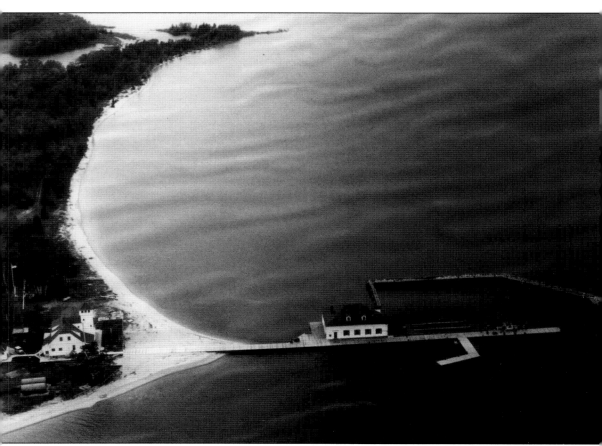

Diesel fuel and lead contamination, frozen water pipes and virtual isolation eventually made the Plum Island Station too costly to man and maintain. In the fall of 1990, the station was relocated to a remodeled chalet on southern Washington Island and renamed Washington Island Station. This station is considered a "station small" under the direction of Sturgeon Bay Canal Station and only manned from Memorial Day to Labor Day. Since abandonment, Plum Island has been the victim of neglect and the elements.

In October 2004, the Coast Guard completed an $863,000 cleanup of lead and fuel contamination. The original three separate Door County Coast Guard stations have now been incorporated into one: Sturgeon Bay Canal Station. This is possible with the advent of modern radio, radar, and boat technologies. There is no longer a need for many stations to search the shores for wrecks as most assistance is requested by radio and occurs off shore. (Courtesy USCG.)

Seven

CURRENT EFFORTS
PRESERVATION AND TOURISM

Lighthouse structural condition shall be maintained in a manner that will preserve the structure for its role as a support and shelter for signals and their related equipment.
—Lighthouse Maintenance Management Manual, U.S. Coast Guard
Commandant Instruction M16500.6A

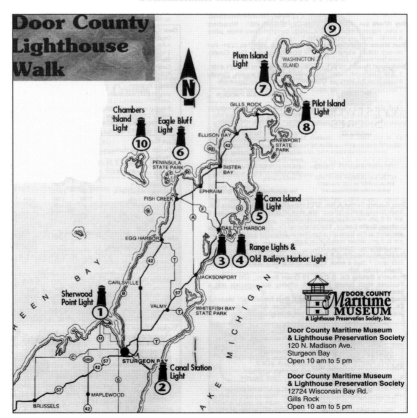

Shown here is a Door County Lighthouse Walk Map. (Courtesy DCMM & LPS.)

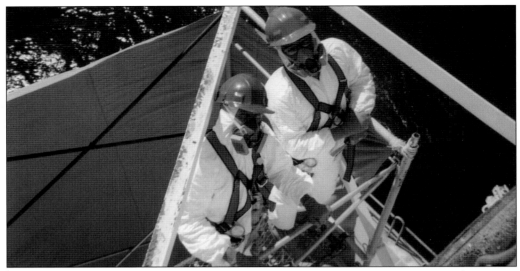

The Coast Guard's role in lighthouse preservation focuses on maintaining structural integrity, protection from the elements, and ensuring the light is functioning properly as an aid to navigation. These photographs were taken during the summer of 2002 as crewmembers of the Cutter *Mobile Bay*, home ported in Sturgeon Bay, prepared the Milwaukee Breakwater Light for paint. Due to lead paint removal, Seaman Charles Castelein (left) and the author Boatswain's Mate Stacy Thomas had to wear glasses, gloves, respirators, and Tyvek suits, as well as safety harnesses and helmets. (Authors' Collection.)

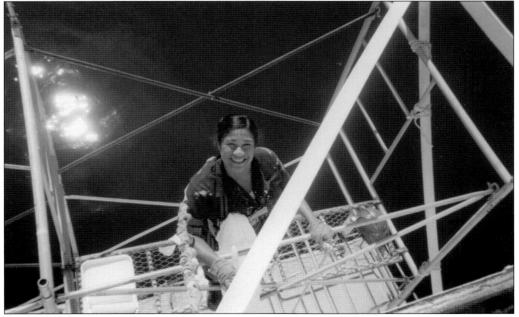

This type of basic maintenance occurs every summer as vessel crews from across the Great Lakes are tasked with augmenting Aids to Navigation Teams (ANT) to complete projects. Once the lead paint is removed and bare metal spots are primed, the structure can be painted as in this photograph of Seaman Mandy Vanden Heuvel. (Authors' Collection.)

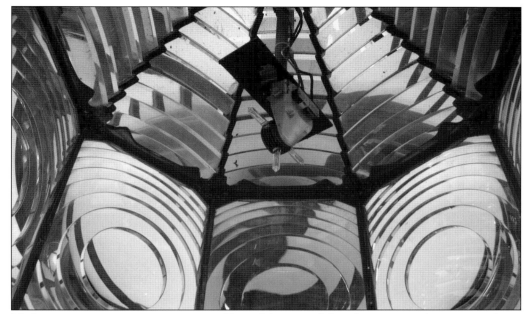

Modernization meant removing some Fresnel lenses, while others received automatic lamp changers which would rotate in a new lamp when one extinguished. The 3rd order lens shown here is still in service in the Sturgeon Bay Canal Light and can cast the light from the amazingly small lamp up to 17 statute miles. (Authors' Collection.)

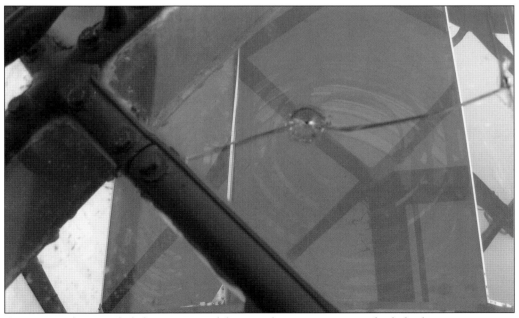

A constant threat to lighthouses is vandalism, such as persons using the light for target practice as shown in this bullet hole in the glass of Sturgeon Bay Canal Light's lantern room. Most visitors to unmanned lights are respectful; however, there are instances of thievery, graffiti, and destruction of property. (Authors' Collection.)

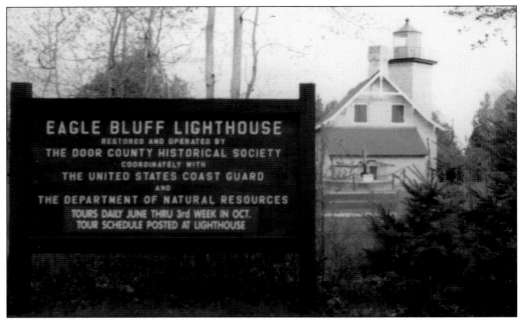

Even though the Coast Guard can only maintain the basic structure and optics, more and more organizations are taking over the historical and cultural elements of lighthouses. The Door County Historical Society chose the Eagle Bluff Lighthouse for restoration in 1960. (Authors' Collection.)

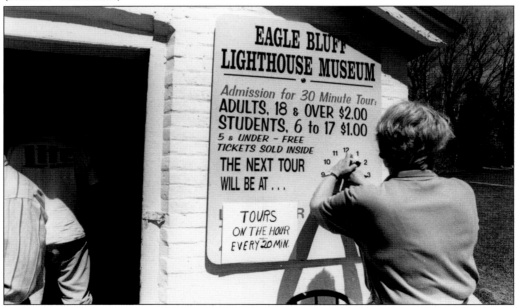

Located in popular Peninsula State Park, the Eagle Bluff Lighthouse Museum is one of the best and easiest lighthouses to visit in the county. In October 2003, the Door County Historical Society took custody of the site from the Wisconsin Department of Natural Resources. This transfer highlights the successful partnership of local, state, and federal entities to preserve nautical heritage. (Courtesy DCMM & LPS.)

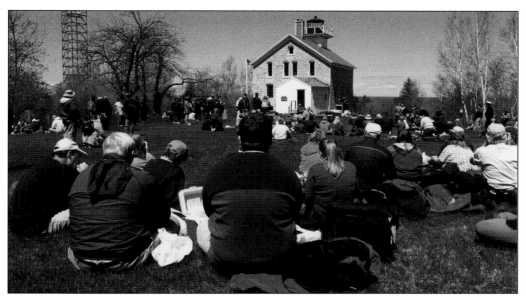

Since 1994, the Friends of Rock Island have undertaken the thorough restoration of Pottawatomie Light. Unlike Eagle Bluff, however, they actually had to fabricate and install a lantern room. A duplicate 4th order Fresnel lens is also being built for installation. Although it requires two ferry rides and a short hike, a visit to this light is extremely rewarding. The dedication of Pottawatomie Lighthouse Museum on May 17, 2004 is captured in this photograph. (Courtesy FORI.)

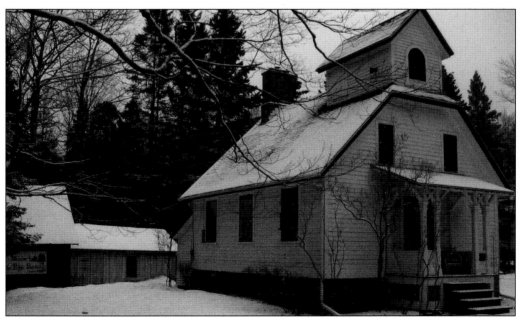

Although the Bailey's Harbor Range has been replaced by a single leading light, the building has received a second life as the office of The Ridges Sanctuary. Since 1937, the nature preserve has provided environmental education and research opportunities. (Authors' Collection.)

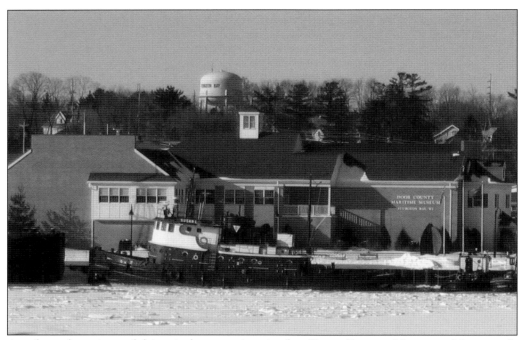

Another champion of historical protection is the Door County Maritime Museum & Lighthouse Preservation Society with sites in Sturgeon Bay, Gills Rock, and Cana Island. (Authors' Collection.)

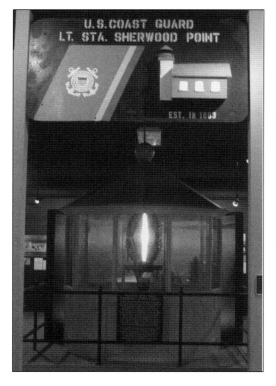

The lighthouse exhibit within the Sturgeon Bay location gives probably the closest and easiest access to an original Fresnel lens. The 4th order lens was in Sherwood Point Light until it was converted to a 300-millimeter lantern in 2002. Ironically, the range of visibility was reduced by one nautical mile due to this conversion. (Authors' Collection.)

The annual Door County Lighthouse Walk, run by the Door County Maritime Museum & Lighthouse Preservation Society, is by far the best way to see the lights. Held each May since 1994, the tour allows access to all the lights, most of which are normally either off limits to the public or not easily accessible. This pamphlet includes an image of Cana Island Light, which the organization has been restoring and operating as a museum. (Courtesy DCMM & LPS.)

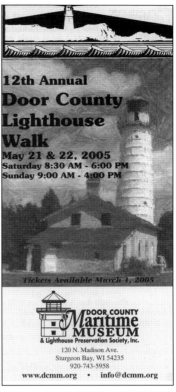

12th Annual Door County Lighthouse Walk
May 21 & 22, 2005
Saturday 8:30 AM - 6:00 PM
Sunday 9:00 AM - 4:00 PM

Tickets Available March 1, 2005

DOOR COUNTY Maritime MUSEUM
& Lighthouse Preservation Society, Inc.
120 N. Madison Ave.
Sturgeon Bay, WI 54235
920-743-5958
www.dcmm.org • info@dcmm.org

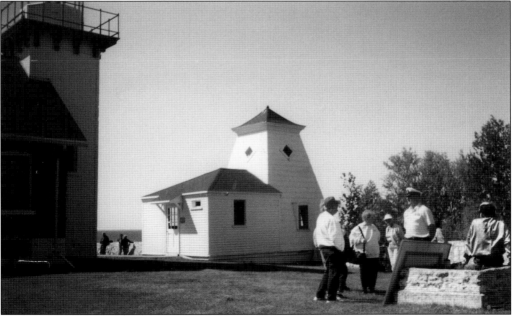

A coastguardsman gives a tour of Sherwood Point Light during the 2000 Door County Lighthouse Walk. The light is off limits the remainder of the year and used as a morale cottage for Coast Guard members and their families. (Courtesy DCMM & LPS.)

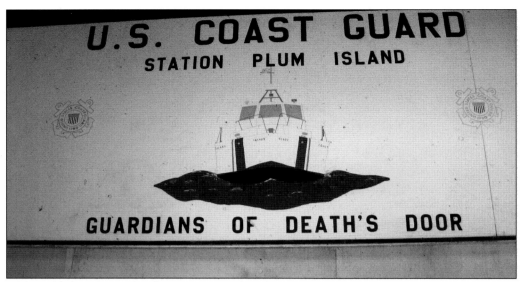

Although the Plum Island Station was abandoned in 1990, the buildings remain on the island and are the center of a current preservation effort. The Jackson Harbor Maritime Museum on Washington Island houses certain artifacts from the station such as this sign. (Authors' Collection.)

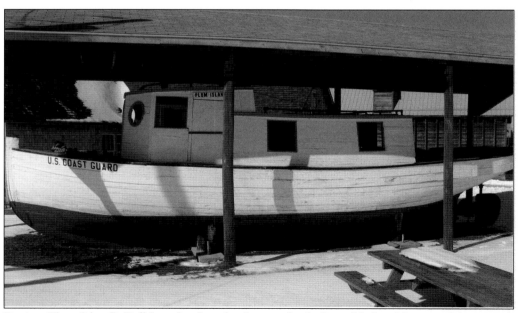

Station Plum Island's *Bull* has also found refuge at the Jackson Harbor Maritime Museum. A roof was built over the boat to help protect it from the elements. (Authors' Collection.)

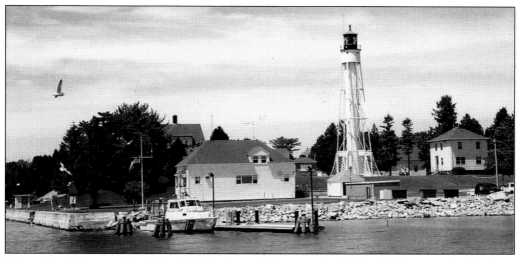

Coast Guard Sturgeon Bay Canal Station is open year-round and thoroughly maintained—some members may say too thoroughly—by active and reserve Coast Guard personnel. During the summer, crewmembers man the seasonal Station (small) Washington Island in Detroit Harbor of that island. (Authors' Collection.)

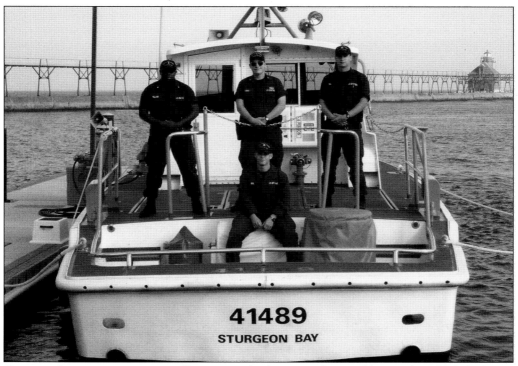

Crewmembers continue to proudly pose with their vessels, just like in the old Life-Saving Service. Pictured from left to right are Machinery Technician Tolliver (boarding officer), author Boatswain's Mate Thomas (coxswain), and Seaman Hall (boat crewman). Fireman Behl (boat engineer) is seated. The 41-foot utility boat, CG 41489, is the workhorse of the station and has been involved in many rescues and law enforcement sorties. (Authors' Collection.)

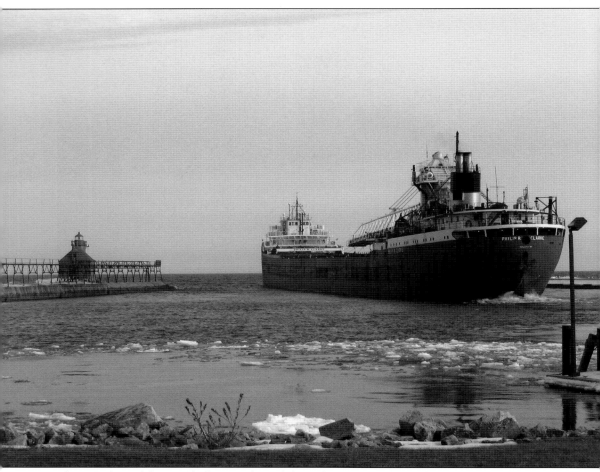

The 767-foot *Philip R. Clarke* is outbound from the Sturgeon Bay Ship Canal in March 2005 after winter lay-up at Bay Shipbuilding Company of Sturgeon Bay. Large vessels still use the canal; however, they are usually without cargo as the canal's 19-foot depth is too shallow. The *Clarke*'s propeller wash is clearly visible as she makes her way past Sturgeon Bay North Pierhead Light. (Authors' Collection.)

Appendix

THE FRESNEL LENS

Developed in 1819 by Frenchman Augustin Jean Fresnel, the lens uses prisms to capture and focus light in one direction. In this way, almost 80% of a light source can be directed towards an observer. Prior to this, reflector systems such as the inefficient Winslow Array were the standard in lighthouses. Fresnel lenses were not put into wide use in U.S. lighthouses until the 1850s, although they had been successfully used elsewhere for decades. (Authors' Collection.)

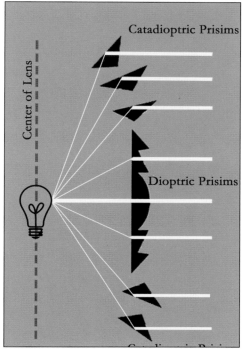

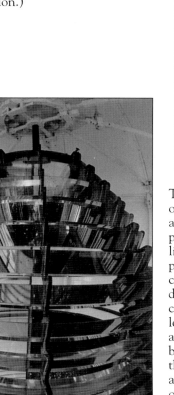

The physics behind a Fresnel lens focuses on prisms joined together to form almost a cocoon around the light source. Dioptric prisms in the center harness and focus the light that passes through them. Catadioptric prisms located above and below the light capture and redirect light in the same direction as the rays passing through the center dioptric prisms. Different orders of lenses were created depending on how far a light needed to be projected. The order is based upon how far the light source is from the lens. A 3rd order lens, such as the one at Cana Island pictured here, has a distance of 19.7 inches from the light to the lens. In Door County, lighthouses had the following lenses: 3rd, 3 1/2, 4th, 5th, and 6th order, ranging from largest to smallest. (Courtesy DCMM & LPS.)

Select Bibliography

Books

Badtke, Frances. *Eagle Lighthouse*. Sturgeon Bay, WI: Door County Publishing Co., 1964.

Johnson, Robert Erwin: *Guardians of the Sea: History of the United States Coast Guard, 1915 to the Present*. Annapolis, MD: Naval Institute Press, 1987.

Kargas, Steven. *Keepers of the Lights: Lighthouse Keepers & Their Families, Door County, Wisconsin—1837–1939*. Ellison Bay, WI: Wm. Caxton Ltd., 2000.

Shanks, Ralph, et al: *U.S. Life Saving Service: Heroes, Rescues, and Architecture of the Early Coast Guard*. Petaluma, CA: Costano Books, 1996.

Stonehouse, Frederick: *Wreck Ashore: U.S. Life-Saving Service Legendary Heroes of the Great Lakes*. Duluth, MN: Lake Superior Port Cities Inc., 1994.

Wardius, Barb & Ken: *Wisconsin Lighthouses: A Photographic & Historical Guide*. Madison, WI: Prairie Oak Press, 2000.

Organizations and Websites

Seeing the Light: http://www.terrypepper.com/lights/index.htm

U.S. Coast Guard Historian's Office: http://www.uscg.mil/hq/g-cp/history/collect.html

U.S. Life-Saving Service Heritage Association: http://www.uslife-savingservice.org/

U.S. Lighthouse Society: http://www.uslhs.org/